Grendel
in John
Novel a

By

Sandra Hiortdahl

Cambridge
Scholars
Publishing

Grendel Recast in John Gardner's Novel and *Beowulf*

By Sandra Hiortdahl

This book first published 2022. The present binding first published 2023.

Cambridge Scholars Publishing

Lady Stephenson Library, Newcastle upon Tyne, NE6 2PA, UK

British Library Cataloguing in Publication Data
A catalogue record for this book is available from the British Library

ISBN (10): 1-5275-1055-7
ISBN (13): 978-1-5275-1055-5

TABLE OF CONTENTS

ACKNOWLEDGEMENTS

I would like to thank my dear friend, Howard C. Dale, who generously created the artwork for the cover of this edition. More of his work may be found at www.howarddale.com

My doctoral dissertation forms the nucleus of this work, completed under a fellowship from The Catholic University of America, and with the superior guidance of my advisor, Dr. Ernest Suarez. At CUA, I also received invaluable help from Dr. Christopher Cain and Dr. Stephen Wright. I am indebted to those who read the earliest versions of this edition and offered their guidance, including Zack Keith and Amy Ramsey Drinnon.

The John Gardner Society of Batavia, New York, provided boundless love, lodging, and kinship, including Marge and Tom Cervone, Jim Fessenden, Helen and John Maier, Phyllis Andrews (University of Rochester, Rare Books & Special Collections), and the founder and longtime helmsman, Charley Boyd. Those closest to John Gardner kindly offered insights on the man himself, including Joel Gardner, Liz Rosenberg, Robert Mooney, and Jan Quackenbush.

I am indebted to my parents, Jack and Stella Hiortdahl, to Gerry Fisher and Barry Barrell, to Linda Cades, to Sophie Kerr—and, as always, to my light and inspiration, the incomparable Danny Lane.

CHAPTER ONE

GRENDEL'S THREE BATTLES

Introduction

Since its publication in 1971, John Gardner's *Grendel* has given readers, educators, and scholars many ideas to debate and ponder. The creation of a hero from the famed first monster in *Beowulf* has made a place for it in college and high school curriculums. With this has come the distinction of being among the most banned novels in the United States. Gardner's prolific writing life, cut short by a tragic motorcycle accident when he was forty-nine, covers wide ground, including creative works, guidebooks for aspiring writers, scholarship, and treatises on the morals of art. As well, his generosity of spirit and passion for literature is reflected in interviews, in the remembrances loved ones, and in readers like myself whose lives have been changed by his legacy.

More specifically, the literary largesse of John Gardner has given rise to innumerable interpretations of his most famous work, *Grendel*.[1] By its nature, the novel is an inversion. Whether such irony reflects Gardner's desire to critique modern society, and if such commentary leads the work toward a postmodern unraveling of the poem's ethical foundations—or if it merely emphasizes them—remains a matter of dispute.

Fueling this debate is the question of how closely we should consider Gardner's heated polemic decrying postmodernism, *On Moral Fiction*, in which he said "The traditional view is that true art is moral: it seeks to improve life, not debase it. It seeks to hold off, at least for a while, the twilight of the gods and us. I do not deny that art, like criticism, may legitimately celebrate the trifling. It may joke, or mock, or while away the time. But trivial art has no meaning or value except in the shadow of more serious art, the kind of art that beats back the monsters and, if you will, makes the world safe for triviality. That art that tends toward destruction,

---

[1] John Gardner, *Grendel* (New York: Vintage Press, 1971). Text references refer to pages in this edition.

the art of nihilists, cynics... is not properly art at all."[2] One may ask whether Gardner considers his novel *Grendel* to be "art" (he does, so the question is, how does it fit?). Further, no one has addressed the scenes in the novel that inspire school boards to ban it, the most horrific being Grendel's sexual assault of Wealtheow in Chapter Seven. Since the *Beowulf* poet never mentions any contact between Grendel and Wealtheow, the added scene in the novel is all the more curious.

Gardner was, of course, fully knowledgeable on *Beowulf* and its scholarship. As well as being a published and respected medievalist, he taught courses in Old English and medieval poetry from his graduate student days until several years before his death in 1982. Gardner's particular fascination was *Beowulf.* The poem was, according to his son Joel, "always a favorite topic of discussion, or the launching pad for a joke . . . Dad could quote it at length, sometimes mixing modern English with Anglo-Saxon just for sport . . . "[3] At the time he published *Grendel*, Gardner was thirty-four. John Howell puts it well, saying that the novel's "resonance suggests that the monster-hero (Grendel) had been lurking in his imagination for some years. By the time he had completed the novel in the summer of 1970, he had been teaching and puzzling over the Anglo-Saxon epic—his source of inspiration—for twelve years."[4]

Gardner's statements that art should be life affirming apply well to *Beowulf.* Ridding the world of mankind's attackers, the hero Beowulf takes on the role of savior, in both the basic sense of adventure hero and in the more allegorical sense. As well, the attackers themselves (Grendel, his mother, and the dragon) represent forces destructive to mankind. Beowulf is thus the moral character while the monsters are either amoral or immoral, depending on one's view of their natures and cosmic alliances. Applying this view of art to Gardner's *Grendel* is trickier, for in this paradigm, isn't Gardner's Grendel the monster who gets beaten back?

For the bulk of the novel, most would agree that the monster narrator does not seek to improve human life. Indeed, Gardner takes pains to emphasize Grendel's brutality. Since the first-person narrative is decidedly slanted against humans, one's choices are either to side with Grendel, and thereby approve of his choices to destroy humans, or to take sides with his adversaries. Given his thorough assessment of them, the latter is no easy task. Either Grendel is right and humans deserve to be destroyed, or he is wrong and their positive qualities, not shown in the novel, would redeem

---

[2] John Gardner, *On Moral Fiction* (New York: Basic Books, 1978), 5

[3] Joel Gardner, interviewed by the author (Annual John Gardner Conference, Susquehanna, PA, 2009)

[4] John M. Howell, *Understanding John Gardner* (Columbia: USC Press, 1993), 61

them. On the surface, neither choice seems to generate much by way of life improvement, as appears in the plot or as one may glean from the experience of reading the novel.

Another challenge comes in locating the book within the scope of Gardner's more traditional novels, most of which have a broad and more optimistic artistic vision. A brief list of the titles of works that center on Gardner's fiction reveals the issue: Cowart's *Arches & Light . . . ,*[5] Morris' *A World of Order and Light . . . ,*[6] Nutter's *A Dream of Peace: Art and Death in the Fiction of John Gardner.*[7] Central tenets such as order, light, and peace go well with Gardner's *October Light*, *Nickel Mountain*, and *Mickelsson's Ghosts*, in which even severe tragedies allow for life affirming truths. *Grendel*, however, begins with a character we know is doomed and leads us first-person through a lifetime of violence and suffering to his fatal end at the hands of Beowulf, where he remains petulant and seemingly unrepentant for his brutality.

Some posit that Gardner means for us to see one of the other characters as the life affirming hero of the story, though this stance has some complications. Others tend to see the book as parody and dark humor, even those who see brilliance, scholars such as John Howell who describes *Grendel* as " . . . Gardner's improvisation and parody."[8] This second view would explain the work's grim and sometimes brutal tone, as well as its inverted form, yet it leaves important questions unanswered.

Howell calls *Beowulf's* Grendel, "merely a symbol of darkness, chaos, and death" while he sees Gardner's Grendel as a "fully realized" character. For Howell, Gardner "deconstructs" and "recasts"[9] the poem. As he views it, Gardner transfers the three battles of *Beowulf* into internal conflicts within Grendel as he struggles with self-identity related to his place in the world, his mother, and his darker self via the dragon (whom Howell sees as a projection of Grendel's consciousness). Howell sees the novel as deconstructing and fully transposing events in the poem from the physical realm to the self-contained, psychological conflicts of Grendel. Such parallels between the poem and the novel had not been explored, nor had the importance of Grendel's psyche.

---

[5] David Cowart, *Arches & Light, The Fiction of John Gardner* (Carbondale: Southern Illinois UP, 1983)

[6] Gregory Morris, *A World of Order and Light: The Fiction of John Gardner* (Athens: U Georgia P, 1984)

[7] Ronald Nutter, *A Dream of Peace: Art and Death in the Fiction of John Gardner* (New York: Peter Lang, 1997)

[8] (Howell, *Understanding John Gardner*, 61-62)

[9] I borrowed this term from Howell, above, for my title.

He doesn't examine correlations between the actual battles in the two works, nor does he explore the ideological conflicts of the poem that Gardner outlines in his scholarly essays on *Beowulf*, including links to Fulgentius and *The Nichomachean Ethics*. Generally speaking, Gardner is more likely than Gardner scholars to explore and applaud the complexities of medieval works, particularly *Beowulf*. The form of the poem, as Tolkien's famous essay "*Beowulf*: The Monsters and the Critics"[10] establishes, has not always been easily classified, so it bears noting that Gardner considered it to be allegorical, though not strictly Christian or Judeo-Christian allegory.

In *The Construction of Christian Poetry in Old English*, Gardner discusses at length the use and adaptation of classical poems and mythologies by Anglo-Saxon poets.[11] Gardner considers it highly likely that thinkers such as Fulgentius influenced Anglo-Saxon tradition by absolving the ancient poets, including Virgil and Homer, of their pagan traditions—this would have left Anglo-Saxon poets free to use, imitate, and copy the forms of these classical stories.

As Gardner describes it, these poets felt they were putting such classical works to good use by more or less translating them into a Christian medium, just as church founders adapted pagan traditions to their purpose. Gardner notes, "A properly religious purpose could justify the preservation of pagan material—to lure men into the church as Aldhelm did with his secular songs, or to dramatize, ornament, or illustrate matters of doctrine" (5).

In *Grendel*, Gardner's inversion of the poem highlights the ironies and the humor, yet if we consider his intentions as more straightforward, as a parallel to those of the *Beowulf* poet, with the very battles themselves corresponding one-to-one, Grendel becomes a modern doppelganger of the poem's mighty hero. When viewed this way, one sees more clearly how to make sense of the novel's seeming bizarre and incongruous anomalies

---

[10] J.R.R. Tolkien, "*Beowulf*: The Monsters and the Critics," *Proceedings of the British Academy*, 22 (1936): 245–95. Reprinted in *An Anthology of Beowulf Criticism*, ed. Lewis E. Nicholson (Notre Dame, Ind.: University of Notre Dame Press, 1963).

[11] John Gardner, *The Construction of Christian Poetry in Old English*. (Carbondale: Southern Illinois University Press, 1975). While *The Construction of Christian Poetry in Old English* was published in 1975, four years after the publication of *Grendel*, the original article from which the book's chapter came, and in which these quotations similarly appear, was published the year before *Grendel*, in 1970, under the title, "Fulgentius's Expositio Vergiliana Continentia and the Plan of *Beowulf*: Another Approach to the Poem's Style and Structure," in *Papers on Language and Literature*, 6 (1970): 227-62.

(those scenes and motifs wholly nonexistent in the poem) that have long stymied readers and scholars. Ultimately, such a reading provides a deeply complex ethical perspective on the work, one which rests compatibly with Gardner's stated views on the role of art and the artist, even as it reveals the truths in Grendel's grimly amusing view of humanity.

If Grendel's story is to contain more resonance than the grim viewpoint of a monster doomed to perish, or a satire on the heroic epic—if indeed it is to be counted as more than a snide comment on Anglo-Saxon value systems or on modern philosophies such as existentialism and nihilism—then it must connect Grendel's experiences to some aspect of the human condition as most people in the modern world perceive it.

And if *Grendel* is to be moral fiction as Gardner has defined it in *On Moral Fiction* and other places, then it must also contain an ethic of life affirmation. In *On Moral Fiction*, he defines it further, "True art is *by its nature* moral. We recognize true art by its careful, thoroughly honest search for and analysis of values. It is not didactic because, instead of teaching by authority and force, it explores open-mindedly to learn what it should teach."[12] Granted, to teach values from the viewpoint of a ferocious and highly irate creature with extraordinary strength and an active imagination is no easy feat, yet Gardner's treatment of morality is neither simple nor neatly resolved in any of his works.

The advantage in the case of *Grendel* is the novel's connections to its Anglo-Saxon predecessor, combined with the considerable scholarly analysis Gardner does of the poem. In *The Construction of Christian Poetry in Old English,* he devotes considerable time to *Beowulf*, noting its relationship to pagan fables, its reliance on Christian motifs, and his vigorous disagreement with scholars who suggested the poem lacked sophistication (53-84). Gardner references not only *Beowulf* itself, but concepts extant to the poem, including religious, philosophical, and folktale motifs, in effect taking these as part and parcel of the original. In the last words of the epilogue, he calls *Beowulf* " . . . the greatest poem in Old English" (120).

An examination of *Grendel* through such a lens shows that it parallels the poem's three famed battles with three battles fought by Grendel. In so doing, it becomes an allegory on the modern human condition. Centering on monstrous Grendel as the hero-anti-hero who wants to be human with every ounce of his being, even at his death, it walks us through his progression from innocence, to depravity, to something perhaps resembling salvation. The issue of identity, particularly as it relates to individuals who

[12] (Gardner, *On Moral Fiction*, 19)

are (or who feel they are) outcast from society, culture, and community, finds resonance in nearly all of Gardner's works. It does in *Grendel* as well, and importantly so.

Grendel's Battles: Overview

An analysis of *Grendel* within a context of Gardner's discussions of *Beowulf* reveals this: each corresponds in specific ways to the three battles fought by Beowulf in the poem. Three distinct attacks differ markedly from the others: they are dramatized rather than referred to in the abstract; Grendel faces counterattack and death in these encounters; during these fights, he experiences the height of emotions, many of which are in conflict, raising the level of drama; in these three instances, the event itself shows a distinct marker of Grendel's progression in his evolving identity. Gardner's design for the novel, more complex than previously recognized, places Grendel within a parallel allegory.

Given this, it makes sense that he'd take a similar approach to *Grendel,* incorporating outside ideas of many types. As does the poem, Gardner's novel establishes meaning through a mixture of allegorical associations and styles. Indeed, his thoughts on the function of allegory in the poem as a purveyor of themes provides insight on the workings of *Grendel's* plot, especially in how the three infamous battles of *Beowulf* are inverted and transposed into three parallel battles fought by Grendel.

He uses Fulgentius' notions of the tripartite soul to divide his novel into these three distinct scenes of battle, with each corresponding to a mixture of arma, virum, or primus.[13] Further, uncovered symbols explain scenes and characters in the novel that do not appear in the poem (some of which have resulted in the novel having been banned at times). I will cover these in more depth as we consider the novel chapter by chapter, but briefly they are as follows, with each corresponding in order to the famed three battles in *Beowulf.*

The first battle may be labeled "Enter a Stranger, Offering Aid," and corresponds to Fulgenitian arma, the force of might, strength, and weapons.

[13] In *The Complete Works of the Gawain Poet*, Gardner clarifies his ideas on man's tripartite soul, "Despite ambiguities in some key words, in Fulgentius' view of arma [virtue], virum [wisdom], and primus [sensuality], one easily recognizes a preoccupation of early Church writers . . . a concern with man's tripartite soul—rational, irascible, concupiscent—analogous to the three-part divine spirit, i.e., Wisdom, Power, Goodness," *The Complete Works of the Gawain Poet*, (Carbondale: Southern Illinois University Press), 230

The poem's scene of Beowulf arriving and doing battle with Grendel corresponds to the novel's Chapter Four, where Grendel enters the human encampment with the dead body over his shoulder and is attacked. Both protagonists are alien to Hrothgar's Danes and pose a threat, though each is known briefly by reputation.

In both, a poet's songs glorify humanity. Nakedness becomes a motif in both scenes, somewhat oddly. In the poem, Beowulf decides to strip off his armor to fight Grendel (though later he doesn't fight Grendel's mother or the dragon in the nude). In the novel, Grendel discovers a naked corpse, though the "nakedness" seems arbitrary (one could understand a thief taking weapons and possessions, but clothing?). In the poem, Beowulf kills Grendel by pulling off his arm at the shoulder; in the novel, Grendel throws the body over his shoulder as he enters, and then the humans attack him with spears.

While Beowulf in the poem is saving the Danes from their adversary, Gardner's Grendel in the novel attempts to save them by pointing out their hypocrisy, begging them in his calls for peace to treat one another with mercy. In each case, the protagonist is an outsider who wishes to be part of Hrothgar's community. While Beowulf is accepted into the clan in the poem, at least on a temporary basis, the opposite happens in the novel. The humans don't understand Grendel's attempt to communicate; they see only a monster lugging a corpse, and so they project the murder onto the "monster" rather than seeing themselves as the perpetrators of violence. This corresponds to Grendel's lack of self-awareness, particularly here, where he fails to anticipate their horror at his appearance.

In the poem, Beowulf wins by virtue of his might (arma), though he chooses to fight in a naked and more vulnerable state, and this magnifies his heroism. By contrast, the denuded corpse that Grendel carries exemplifies the dishonor of the humans who regularly commit crimes against one another. Though Grendel is unarmed and calling for peace and mercy, they attack him. He loses and must flee as a result of human arma (their weapons and spears), though his concern about the human community's values shows loyalty, a positive virum. Note that he carries the corpse over his shoulder, not desecrating it by dragging it on the ground; in the poem, Beowulf kills Grendel by tearing off his arm at the shoulder. Brazenly, he hangs it over the mantle as his trophy.

Furthering the connection between the two works, what follows this first battle in the poem is a digression celebrating Beowulf's victory, a story that glorifies Sigemund the dragon slayer. In the novel, after Grendel's first violent encounter with humans in Chapter Four, a long digression follows (Chapter Five), that consists almost entirely of the

Dragon's speech. The Dragon glorifies the notion of Grendel becoming a monster. We see Gardner inverting the poem to match his inverted allegory, but here the inversion is the outsider's failed attempt to bring peace, whereas in the poem Beowulf's slaying of Grendel does bring some peace. While Beowulf's heroism is lauded, the humans in the novel reject Grendel because of his otherness.

The second attack in both the poem and the novel may be labeled, "Lair of the Queen, the Maternal Feminine," a parallel between Beowulf's fight with Grendel's mother and *Grendel* Chapter Seven, Grendel's sexual assault of Wealtheow. In each work, the protagonist enters the lair of a female who represents the mother of his enemies, and in each case the attack is alarmingly physical, with an emphasis on sexuality. *Beowulf* scholars (specifically Jane Chance, with whose work Gardner was familiar), point out the sexuality in the poem when Beowulf and Grendel's naked mother grapple on the floor. This parallels the novel's sexual assault on Wealtheow by Grendel, and it explains much more satisfactorily than did the notion of Gardner using the attack simply to show Grendel's brutality. As well, there is correspondence to the Fulgentian idea of primus, a term which Gardner refers to as "sensuality."[14]

While Grendel in the novel refers to Wealtheow's bloody sexual organs and says in retrospect that he used the image to cure himself (of his attraction to her, one assumes),[15] in the poem the fiery blood of Grendel's mother melts Beowulf's sword (swords as another image of sexuality, so a melted sword would symbolize the loss of erection).[16] Finally, while Beowulf leaves the slain dam and cuts off Grendel's head as a trophy, in the novel, Grendel leaves Wealtheow alive but kills her brother's pet bear by squeezing it to death (a symbolic connection to motifs to do with Beowulf and bears). In each case, the attacker's win is not symbolized by victory over the mother, but by enacting a virtual death of one's foil.

The result of Beowulf's loyalty in fighting this second battle is his acceptance into Hrothgar's community. In *Grendel*, the result is the monster having proven the cowardly humans incapable of defending their queen. Virum as positive (Beowulf the hero), inverted virum (Grendel's mother's loyalty to her son), and lack of virum (the humans in the novel) are highlighted. Here, however, we see Grendel's progression in identity

---

[14] (Gardner, *The Complete Works of the Gawain Poet*, 230)

[15] (Gardner, *Grendel*, 115)

[16] For a recent essay on this well-known motif in Medieval studies, see Rachel E. Savini, "The —ick of It: Phalluses, Swords, and Character Development in *Beowulf* and *Morte d'Arthur*," *International Journal of Undergraduate Research and Creative Activities*, Vol. 11, Article 7. (2019) DOI: 10.7710/2168-0620.1135

from a rejected outsider to a creature adopting the definition placed on him by the ruling culture and, ironically, proving his dominance over that culture.

The third attack in the poem and the novel results in the death of our protagonists. Beowulf in the poem kills and is killed by the dragon, while Grendel in Chapter Twelve of the novel is killed by Beowulf (who inexplicably grows wings and breathes fire, like a dragon). In each case, the death is preceded by a period of time in which the protagonist has been at the zenith of their station, or primus. Yet, each has grown old and weary, ignoring premonitions of death as well as the advice of those who urge caution. Notions of doom and fate prevail. Beowulf in the poem talks to his men on the cliff, while Grendel in the novel dies on the cliff's edge surrounded by animals.

Fulgentian "virum," loyalty of wisdom gained through life experience, would seem to lead both protagonists toward this acceptance of death as an inevitability that comes with the waning of strength (arma) and position (primus), yet ironically also, in lacking wisdom, both Beowulf in the poem and Grendel in the novel come to their deaths more quickly and violently than they might otherwise. In the poem, Beowulf seems hopeful that the dragon's treasure will help his people, when in fact it's useless. In the novel, Grendel claims he has died by "accident," even as he insults the animals gathered to watch him die.

As the examination of these corollaries to *Beowulf* shows, John Gardner's *Grendel* is not merely an existential satire on an Anglo-Saxon poem but instead an infusion of allegorical connections designed to recreate and reinvent the structure he saw in the original, even as he inverted the protagonist. As well, Gardner's use of intertextual blending makes significant points concerning cultural alterity, identity, and the role of community. The famed first monster of English literature becomes, at the hands of John Gardner, the modern hero made antihero by the culture that outcasts him.

Grendel, Chapter One, Surveying the Text

Gardner opens his novel with Grendel approaching the end of his twelve-year reign. He sees the world as without a creator: "The sun spins *mindlessly* overhead, the shadows lengthen and shorten as if by plan" (7), a mantra repeated throughout the novel. In several instances, Grendel comments on natural and man-made elements that he sees as evidence for the lack of a guiding force in the universe. Grendel culminates with this, "The cold night air is reality at last: indifferent to me as a stone face carved on a high wall to show that the world is abandoned" (9). As one can see, Grendel's interaction with the world shows the order of it to be, in his opinion, without any intelligible, or communicating, higher force. Further, Grendel knows that his creation of the world through thought and language is not the actual world. He recognizes, on some level, how his dialogue has no hearer but himself, and so his creation of a false world manipulates no one except himself.

In this way, he claims himself as his only audience, yet suffers as a result of his aloneness. This aloneness may be seen, then, as a delusion which traps him into ignoring his identity. Several times in succession he repeats variations on the phrase, "Talking, talking. Spinning a web of words . . . " (8). Rather beginning the novel with "cub" Grendel in Chapter Two, Gardner gives us the monster in all of its glory, that is nonetheless a structured reinvention of the poem's Grendel, this one with language, philosophical concepts, and a sense of humor, though with the same tendencies toward savage violence.

Scholars have noted how the symbol of the ram and the designation of the month as April connect it both to Chaucer's *Canterbury Tales* and T.S. Eliot's *The Wasteland*.[17] As well, several scholars have analyzed the novel's use of astrology, with each chapter containing a symbol and idea from signs of the zodiac, progressing in order from Aries (Chapter One) to Pisces (Chapter Twelve). Gardner himself mentions it in an interview with Joe David Bellamy and Pat Ensworth, suggesting a "clue" to unraveling the novel's core.[18] Barry Fawcett and Elizabeth Jones in "The Twelve Traps in John Gardner's Grendel"[19] and Craig J. Stromme's "The Twelve Chapters of Grendel"[20] also provide excellent studies. Per Winther finds the actual connections less than convincing what he categorizes as an overall scheme of inclusion and description, what he terms Gardner's "collage technique."[21]

A more detailed look at the allusions may provide insight as well on Grendel's search for identity. The ram's appearance in the novel is certainly a representation of Aries the Ram, as many have noted, yet there is irony in the "start" of the novel and the "start" of the astrological year

---

[17] (Howell, *Understanding John Gardner*, 65)

[18] Joe David Bellamy and Pat Ensworth, "John Gardner" in *Conversations with John Gardner*, edited Allan Chavkin (University of Mississippi Press, 1990), 6-27.

[19] Barry Fawcett and Elizabeth Jones, "The Twelve Traps in John Gardner's Grendel" (*American Literature* 62, no. 4, 1990), 634–47

[20] Craig J. Stromme, "The Twelve Chapters of *Grendel*" (*Critique: Studies in Modern Fiction* 20.1, 1978) 83-92

[21] (Winther, *The Art of John Gardner*, 7)

coming at the "end" of Grendel's life and near the end of his reign as terrible monster. The motif serves several purposes, first in its establishment of the zodiac frame, second as an extension of this an ironic "beginning" to Grendel's "end," and third in its homage to both Chaucer and Eliot. Fourth, I would suggest, is the correlation of the fairly trendy notion of the zodiac (popular as a motif in the 1970's when Gardner writes *Grendel*) with the literary greats of the past, showing his delight in blending the modern with the classics.

The ram serves several other purposes. The suggestion from Grendel's point of view would seem to be a metaphoric alignment of the ram with Hrothgar, and in some ways, of course, the end of Grendel's reign would mean a new beginning for Hrothgar and the Danes, a new springtime engendered by Beowulf. The ram responds to Grendel's yelling thus, "He cocks his head like an elderly, slow-witted king, considers the angles, decides to ignore me" (5), and this produces more antagonism in the monster. Still, the old ram/king refuses to acknowledge Grendel's supremacy, even when a supernatural element is added, "I shake my two hairy fists at the sky and I let out a howl so unspeakable that the water at my feet turns sudden ice and even I myself am left uneasy" (5). The water turning to ice adds a fabulist twist to the novel, though this is not followed up with much intensity as the chapter continues.[22]

Leaving the scene, Grendel immediately begins to distinguish himself from the ram, which he regards as a creature motivated to obstinacy by natural urges. In this way we have a lovely reversal, as the human (Hrothgar) is represented by a creature suffering from grossly animal instincts, while the monster narrator feels only disgust at the lack of "dignity." The humor is inherent, yet pathos comes when one considers Grendel's situation. His anger and disgust notwithstanding, he is nonetheless a sentient creature whose physical reactions to the spring time in the form of lust can have no outlet in the form of a mate, as, in the novel as well as the poem, it would seem the only other creature of his kind is his mother. If there are creatures of his kind, he and his mother apparently have abandoned them, for the poem specifies, "he lived for a time in the home of the *monsters'* race,"[23] the suggestion being that he used to live in

[22] By contrast, even when we return to this point in time in Chapter 12, Grendel's attack on the goat is realistic in detail.

[23] E. Talbot Donaldson, *trans*., *Beowulf: A New Prose Translation* (New York: W.W. Norton, 1966), 5. I am using E. Talbot Donaldson's prose translation because Gardner references it within his own translation of the poem. In a handwritten sheet entitled "Notes on translation" is the quotation of lines 53-4, prefaced with the word "Lit" (literal) and followed by the note, "E.T. Donaldson's

the land of his own race, but now lives in a land distinct from them, the land of the humans.

This isolation from creatures, nature, and God as seen in a personified and uncaring universe, creates self-pity in Grendel which he recognizes in himself and proceeds to mock, addressing himself as he rants. The stream of consciousness spins outward to an assumed audience. Within such a milieu one sees a number of humorous contexts but, it must also be allowed, a considerable development of Grendel's character, and, in particular, his desire to define himself. While this situation is ironic and not without humor, it carries an undercurrent of seriousness pertaining to his position as outcast intent on finding an audience.

Nor does Gardner shy from giving his readers the full context of Grendel's violent leanings. In Grendel's descriptions of the world, readers are lured in with lyrical depictions and literary allusions, only to have the effect reversed with dreadful images of violence "The tender grasses peek up, innocent yellow, through the ground: the children of the dead" (an allusion to Walt Whitman), then, "(It was just here, this shocking green, that once when the moon was tombed in clouds, I tore off sly old Athelgard's head)"(7). In the first two and a half pages of the novel, Gardner establishes a story brimming with narrative complexities and allusions, both a modern monster story based on a heroic poem and an examination of the relation between perception and truth.

Grendel's isolation prompts a stream of consciousness which at times traps him within his monomaniacal perspective, thus pointing to the inherent dangers of isolationism in general and existentialism in particular. As well, the role of the imagination in constructing any individual's personal perspective enters here. Grendel's first-person narration contains within it the issues of all first-person narratives, intensified by tendencies toward fancy, exaggeration, and violent madness. However, this does not mean that Gardner wants his readers to see Grendel's essential perceptions of the world—and humankind in particular—as faulty. While the monster does indeed display unique views and monstrous attitudes, nonetheless he is, at base, a reliable narrator in the customary understanding of this: his accounts of events and people, while perhaps skewed, are neither lies nor hallucinations.

The central conflict is Grendel's total isolation: nature itself and its creatures are seen as separate; anything like a plan or scheme in the cosmos seems ridiculous to him, including the idea of a god; his mother,

---

translation" (from Box 25-7, the first of five pages of handwritten notes explaining Gardner's translation choices, Special Collections, John Gardner, University of Rochester Library). It's also inexpensive and fairly accessible to students.

his only kin, cannot communicate in language with him; even the humans, with whom he would seem to have the most in common, are objects of his scorn and at any rate, by the end of his twelve-year reign of terror, are at war with him. He describes it this way, "Such are the tiresome memories of the shadow-shooter, earth-rim-roamer, walker of the world's weird wall" (7), a succession of kennings that pay tribute to Anglo Saxon poetry, just as they are an ironic nod toward the narrator's sardonic commentary. Grendel's constant inner conversations show not just a propensity for weird humor and sudden philosophical contemplation, but also his fragmented personality.

Grendel's discussion of his mother raises questions (also in the poem) concerning their species, and, as well, the alliance of humankind with guilt, and by extension to Cain's sin. At the same time, the opening makes clear Grendel's distinction from animals, none of whom accept him as one of their own. Nor can Grendel be merely human, for his physical prowess far surpasses any of Hrothgar's thanes. Chapter One contains a description of Grendel's mead hall raids, the horror made humorous by how the thanes cover the light in an attempt to gain advantage. This blinds *them*, but not Grendel. The humor is not merely in seeing the poem's mead hall raids from an inverted perspective, but in the ironic truths this gives about ourselves, of such errors in our own lives. Attempting to turn situations to our advantage, in our haste we worsen our predicament.

Nor is Grendel exempt from this, for he, too, has human tendencies. In Chapter One, we find him on the eve of his death, sick from power after eleven years of bloodlust. The pinnacle of power has made his existence hellish. At the chapter's ending, the monster stands watching the funeral pyre from a distance, engorged by his night of feasting. He overhears the humans crying out, even in their pain trying to rationalize the horror, suggesting punishment sent by an angry god, that their pain is a result of their own sins (13), references to guilt that mirror his earlier joke about his mother's guilt and humanness. The reference is magnified by his description of the humans as "lunatic" (twice), just as earlier he'd described himself as a "disfigured son of lunatics" (6).

Gardner's monster, while removed from society enough to observe our foibles, nonetheless spends his existence obsessed with the humans he destroys. His inability to master the humans angers him, but the result seems to be a return to his primal self, with "cringe" signifying his sense of guilt, "clawing" his animal-like nails, and "flee for home" (14) a sense of fear along with displacement from the human community—their "home" cannot be his home, for they regard him as "other," and in his reaction to this state, he has further outcast himself by becoming their vanquisher.

The question might be posed: why *shouldn't* Grendel act like a monster? Even in *Beowulf*, the poet gives us terrible Grendel doomed to Hell, yet the creature does not attack randomly. He endures the sounds of the mead hall until he can't any longer. Despite the rage in Grendel's subsequent attack, the *Beowulf* poet seems to imbue the monster with very human qualities of anguish, jealousy, and the desire for power. The poet shows even more empathy to Grendel's mother, noting her loyalty and the fact that she has lost her only son; she may kill Aescher, but she doesn't take his head as a trophy. Instead, she retrieves her son's arm from over the mantle and takes it to her lair with the rest of his remains.

The issue of whether these monsters are human begs the question of who has labeled them inhuman. The poet references Cain and the Old Testament. In our modern world, the parables of Jesus (such as the Good Samaritan) teach love and acceptance, even outside of one's clan. Indeed, stigmatizing others as "less than human" has resulted in the worst of modern atrocities, so why should those forced into such roles honor the human rights of their persecutors?

Grendel's and his mother's associations with Cain and Cain's kin are, in and of themselves, reason in the poem for their disassociation from God. Similarly, both species and race are important considerations in Gardner's novel, as Grendel attempts to define himself and make a place in the world. There exists, then, the basic inquiry into the extent of Grendel's humanness, a significant issue for many reasons but certainly vital when it comes to the issue of whether his "eating people" equates to cannibalism and murder.

Gardner's scholarship on *Beowulf* may be useful here, for the establishment of both an actual and an allegorical frame for the novel. He points to the importance of Scyld's funeral as a motif of the poem's opening and mentions the possible reasons for this funeral as "the formal balance of Beowulf's funeral and Scyld's."[24] Gardner uses a similar paradigm in the novel, the human funeral here in Chapter One, with its anguish of defeat turning into something like relief, as a parallel to Grendel's death in Chapter Twelve at the hands of the human hero, a painful death that is also a respite from suffering.

Chapter One of *Grendel*, for all the humor and irony and indeed a burlesque of rollicking prose, establishes Grendel as a narrator with an important story to tell. His story, beginning near the end of his monstrous

---

[24] (Gardner, *The Construction of Christian Poetry in Old English*, 66)

attacks on Hrothgar's Danes, defines a monster both terrifying and very human. Within this darkly humorous ironic reversal, however, the novel contains many layers, resonances, and parallels, suggesting more than a simple turnabout of a familiar work—indeed, showing it to be Gardner's reinvention of the poem on a modern level.

Grendel, Chapter Two, Surveying the Text

Gardner alludes to Scyld's funeral in Chapter One, so in Chapter Two when he takes readers back to Grendel's childhood, it bears resemblance to *Beowulf's* opening, the mention of Scyld as a foundling. In the novel, Grendel leaves the safety of his home environment and ventures from the cave, for the first time going through the fire-snake lake to the world at the other side. There (completely alone, as infant Scyld was alone once he was put forth in the boat), Grendel is found by men just as Scyld was found by men. The humans in both works spend time staring at the foundling, wondering what they have come upon, and considering the portents.

The men adopt Scyld and he grows into a leader who will become famous as a king who terrifies other tribes by wrecking their mead halls; in Gardner's novel, Grendel the foundling is attacked by humans, rescued by his mother, and grows into the being known as the destroyer of mead halls. In the poem, inclusion in the community creates through fealty, "a good king," while in the novel, alienation of the foundling creates a deadly enemy. Chapter Two parallels the poem both in motif and in theme and becomes a fitting prelude to the rest of the book.

Chapter Two again makes mention of Grendel's skill and use of language, yet the irony here comes both in the reader's apprehension of the words and Grendel's equation of them with non-reality, death and isolation: "Talking, talking, spinning a spell, pale skin of words that closes me in like a coffin," Gardner adds a playful wink to the reader, with "I used to play games when I was young—it might as well be a thousand years ago," since the modern audience is reading a novel written roughly a thousand years after the writing of the poem.

Questions of Grendel's species emerge. Gardner describes child Grendel in terms that connect him to both human children and the offspring of animals: playing "war games," yet "Like a puppy nipping, preparing for battle with wolves" (16). Likewise, within his mother's cave he encounters strange beings that he assumes are in some way related to him; they suggest elements of his heritage, both an alliance to his mother and himself in terms of their glowing eyes, and a connection to humanity through what would seem to be a type of language.

Gardner may be connecting these to the *Beowulf* poet's description of Cain's kin, as described by Donaldson, "From him [Cain] sprang all bad breeds, trolls and elves and monsters—likewise the Giants who for a long time strove with God: He paid them their reward for that."[25] This family connection between Grendel and the cave dwellers may be seen as his community, an idea presented by the zodiac sign corresponding to this chapter, Taurus the bull, a creature that shows up by instinct to protect the calf.

Once injured by the bull, Grendel in immense pain remembers those who share a cave with him and with his mother. In that moment, he seems to recognize their lack of a bond to one another and to him. These and those that follow seem to inspire his existentialist philosophy, the idea that he alone exists in the universe.[26] While Chapter Two is framed by the bull's attack and his mother's rescue of him, its core is Grendel's first encounter with men, who are distinctly separate from animals like the bull and creatures like himself and his mother, in terms of physical attributes and in their response to danger.

In a humorous scene as the humans surround Grendel in the tree and wonder what he is, whether fungus or spirit. Their fearful response when he cries out in hunger shows the language barrier, but also suggests Grendel's inability to perceive himself as men perceive him, as a threat. In Gardner's scenario, had the monster been more prudent or the men more courageous, an entirely different outcome may have ensued. Instead, Hrothgar throws an axe, a moment which becomes a focal point in Grendel's memory.

Grendel's mother rescues him, a display of her loyalty foreshadowing her raid on the mead hall after Grendel's death, in the poem. The maternal salvation contains the use of Eucharistic imagery, "Then her smell poured in like blood into a silver cup" (27-28), a comparison that connects his mother to Wealtheow's role in the poem as peace-weaver, emphasized in the novel by a later description of the queen, "When drunken men argued . . . she came between them, wordless, uncondemning, pouring out mead like a mother's love . . . " (103). The pairing of Wealtheow with Grendel's mother will figure largely into the second battle, Chapter Seven.

Rescued by his mother and back in the cave, Grendel comments on the conspicuous absence of the creatures who share their dwelling. Then, though his mother has saved him from probable death at the hands of the humans, he comments instead on her lack of language and her inability to

---

[25] (Donaldson, *trans., Beowulf,* 5)

[26] Howell notes that Grendel's tree incident is the beginning of the character's existentialism (67).

communicate with him verbally (28), mirroring his failed communication with the humans who surrounded him.

The chapter concerns loyalty and protection, tribal unity, attributes of virum, pitted against the might of arma. The bull comes to the calf, seen in the way Hrothgar and his men gather, regroup for protection, and attack, and then shown as Grendel's mother rescues him from both the natural world (the tree, the bull) and the world of humans. When cub Grendel roars from hunger, they halt all discussion and attack, as Hrothgar has ordered, despite the creature being incapacitated in the tree, thus a failure of arma through paranoid fear of danger. It also concerns Grendel's isolation and his need to craft an identity of self-protection; having left the safety of the cave in a sign of independence, he finds himself trapped. In each of the motifs, Grendel pits himself against definitions and spins himself a skin as he attempts to create his own identity (from his past) or to justify it (in the present).

On a wider scale, Grendel's encounter with men separates him from human society, their fearful reaction and attack defining him as monstrous, an ironic contrast to Scyld's adoption by men. Scyld's funeral is compared to his arrival, "They provided him no lesser gifts, treasure of the people, than those had done who at his beginning first sent him forth on the waves, a child alone."[27] Scyld's family provided a presentation which affected his finders in a positive way, and he grows to be a great king and dies with great tributes, as well as the code of kingship that he bequeaths to his sons and their sons. In Grendel's family, the physical traits inherited from his mother, combined with the desire to communicate from his more human ancestry, inspire terror in Hrothgar's court. As a consequence of this first encounter, Grendel sees himself as completely isolated in the world.

That he grows into a brutal killer cannot be attributed to his mother, for she does not use her power until her cub is in danger and her instincts are aroused. In the poem, Grendel raids the mead hall for twelve years, but his mother does not appear except after his death, to avenge him through one death only and to reclaim part of his body. Nor does she reappear: Beowulf must go to her lair to find her. This shifts the blame for Grendel's jealousy and his hunger for dominance away from her and onto his environment, his experiences, and to the human community at large, genetically through Cain and practically, in the Danes' rejection of him.

It does more than this, as well. Just as the use of first-person narration gives Grendel a unique voice, Chapter Two's introduction to Grendel's childhood shows the radical changes he's been through since his time as

---

[27] (Donaldson, *trans., Beowulf*, 4)

an innocent cub. Beowulf arrives well after these changes, so the novel's tension does not come from the disparity between so-called monstrosity and so-called heroism. Rather, both the conflicts and the humor in the novel result from the human community's failures to see beyond their initial perception of him as a hideous creature. They project monstrosity onto him and then, in attempting to fight their perceived foe, they "create" a monster from what might otherwise be a harmless, sentient being.[28] Unfortunately for him, and for the humans he comes to destroy, he takes as his teachers the humans themselves.

In terms of the natural versus the supernatural, while Chapter One shows Grendel as supreme and even charmed, as when on the first page his roar turns the puddle "sudden ice" (5), elements of magical realism are largely absent in Chapter Two, where Gardner gives us "Grendel the cub" as a lovable and endearing character. If Gardner, following this line of thought, creates a novel that inverts the overall perspective, and then in Chapter Two shows us the creature's childhood innocence, either he means for us to discount the innocence as part of the joke—and therefore to see Grendel as a completely biased and unreliable narrator—or he means to point out the actual significance of such a conversion.

Further, in chapters following Two, Grendel finds the humans to be increasingly pathetic. His judgments become harsher. If one assumes he's an untrustworthy narrator, then the core of the book is basically a treatise against unwise Grendel who has lied about his original innocence and likewise is lying about the idiocy of humans. The point of such a novel would be that monsters cannot properly perceive humans, which strikes me as less interesting on all counts.

The movement back in time of Chapter Two echoes in certain ways Gardner's ideas about the poem and its structure. In *The Construction of Christian Poetry in Old English*, he notes the importance of referencing Beowulf's credentials in his development as a hero worthy of great tales: "The poet sets up the terms of the heroic ethic (Fulgentius' principles of felicity) . . . the *Beowulf*-poet shows, through allusions to the hero's past, how Beowulf came to present maturity, the unambiguous state of wisdom and valor from which, in his last days, he will decline."[29]

In Chapter Two of his novel, Gardner begins a similar exploration of how Grendel becomes monstrous. A Fulgentian classification may be applied. His childhood exploits test his arma, perhaps akin to the poem's

[28] Nor is such a proposal absent from the poem: the horror of Grendel's (and his mother's) attacks comes from their connection to humanity, not their distance from it, as Tolkien shows in "*Beowulf*: The Monsters and the Critics," 247

[29] (Gardner, *The Construction of Christian Poetry in Old English*, 77)

stories of Beowulf's contests with Brecca. Likewise, the monster cub struggles to attain virum (loyalty and wisdom), so adopts existentialism as his creed, which makes sense as he is locked out from the human community and has no outlet for communication, no one to help him correct any lapses in logic. Such lapses cause him to perceive himself as completely alone, at direct odds with the bond he may be entitled to on the most natural level, his relationship with his mother. By failing to see himself accurately, Grendel enters into a state of confusion which pulls him back and forth between wanting to belong and wanting to isolate.

Seeing the distinct worlds in the incident with the bull and with the humans, he cannot locate himself, except to ally with his mother's race. Yet this, too, is unsatisfactory. Connections of "blood" figure dramatically into this chapter, so it is fitting for Grendel to end his thoughts with a return to the ideas of speech in the chapter's opening, the speech act being one of the ways he is separate from his mother, and to return to their vital connection through the blood relationship, "I smell my mama's blood and, alarmed, I hear from the walls and floor of the cave the booming, booming of her heart" (29).

Grendel Chapter Three, Surveying the Text

Insofar as Grendel has defined himself in Chapter Two as separate from man, in terms of his interest in conservation and his lack of cruelty (neither killing needlessly nor upsetting the balance of nature), most readers are hard-pressed to disagree with the notion of him as a higher form of being. Grendel describes Hrothgar and his men as, "They were small . . . yet in some ways they were like us, except ridiculous and, at the same time, mysteriously irritating, like rats. Their movements were stiff and regular, as if figured by logic" (24).

The division becomes ironic, the poem's monster now a concerned protector of the natural world while its human heroes figure their movements "by logic" and misuse the environment. Such questions are intensified in Chapter Three, when the Shaper's art creates a myth-like nexus between the heroic marauders of the past and the exploits of Hrothgar's court.

Chapter Three corresponds to the zodiac sign of Gemini the twins, and along with the motif of twins comes our introduction of the Shaper, the poet who inspires the humans by singing of their connection to God.[30] The

---

[30] Gardner names him the "Shaper" after the Anglo-Saxon word *scop*, which means to shape or create, a word also applied to Anglo-Saxon poets.

Shaper "sings for his supper," in the novel, a dual nature consistent with the sign. His songs set up the dynamic inspiring Grendel's first violent entry into Hrothgar's court, in both poem and novel, so his place in the works bears exploration.

While Chapters One and Two may be said to contrast Grendel's ferocious last years with his innocent beginnings, Chapter Three leads us into the middle section of the tale, the events which link the beginning to the ending. They explain his having gone from innocence to anguish, from sanity to madness. The introduction of the Shaper in this chapter further strains Grendel's identity issues, for he is both drawn to and repulsed by the Shaper's art. The Shaper's songs influence Hrothgar's community and strengthen the pride that instigates their nation-building. In addition, his songs become both a religious focal point and a concretization of the creed of conquering.

By contrast, Grendel's complex thought processes find no outlet except in his own "spinning of webs," and he has no members of his species with whom to share them, further drawing him toward the Shaper's art and the humans served by it. Matters are made worse for Grendel by the glorification of humans in the Shaper's songs, especially as those songs prompt Hrothgar's thanes to more bloody warfare. Nor is the influence limited to the humans. Unfortunately for Grendel, the songs prompt him toward a definition of himself as monstrous. So, in effect, the Shaper's art shapes Grendel by teaching him (or seeming to teach him) about monsters and heroes, and codes of behavior to do with both.

Especially here, where Grendel gives us the Shaper's introduction, the facts of the matter must be scrutinized. Examination of the chronology reveals the Shaper's art to be the root cause of Grendel's attack (just as it is in the poem). Gardner's commentary on *Beowulf* underscores this point, "The focus of the lines introducing Grendel is on the monster's sorrowing rage."[31] It isn't clear in the poem how well Grendel understands language, but in the novel, he is entirely capable.

As well, Grendel is poised for a conversion against the humans before the Shaper arrives; the violent "busy ness" of Hrothgar and his men mingles with his own coming of age. As Grendel continues to watch in horrified fascination, year by year, his distaste grows. He comments, "There was nothing to stop the advance of man. Huge boars fled at the click of a harness. Wolves would cower in the glens like foxes when they caught the deadly scent. I was filled with a wordless, obscurely murderous unrest" (40). Up to this point, then, the monster has not attacked. The next

[31] (Gardner, *The Construction of Christian Poetry in Old English*, 66)

sentence heralds the arrival of the new Shaper, "One night, inevitably, a blind man turned up at Hrothgar's *temporary* mead hall," (40, italics mine). The great Heorot has not been built.

Chronologically speaking, Grendel has his first encounter with men as a cub, and although he bears some resentment for Hrothgar's axe attack (the sarcasm of comparing Hrothgar to stepping on a poisonous snake is clear), he does not begin to attack. He watches and his anger grows. Next, the Shaper arrives while Hrothgar is yet in a "temporary" mead hall. The Shaper's first song begins, "Lo, we have heard the honor of the Speardanes, nation-kings, in days now gone, how those battle-lords brought themselves glory . . . " (42), lines which are also the beginning of *Beowulf* the poem. At the same time, the Shaper cannot properly be reciting *Beowulf* because the monster has not yet attacked, nor is there any Heorot, practically speaking, to be attacked. Scyld's story is enough, however, to inspire his audience.

The image of Gemini and duality comes to the fore here, both as a symbol of communication and of dualism. Grendel describes the Shaper as follows: "He knew his art. He was king of the Shapers . . . That was what had brought him over wilderness, down blindman's alleys of time and space, to Hrothgar's famous hall. He would sing the glory of Hrothgar's line and gild his wisdom and stir up his men to more daring deeds, for a price" (42).

The effect on Hrothgar's people is impressive, "They would seize the oceans, the farthest stars, the deepest secret rivers in Hrothgar's name! . . . It went on and on, a fire more dread than any visible fire" (43). Is Grendel wrong to see the inspiration as detrimental? He, too, is affected by the song and begins to perceive a dual reality, the truth he knows to be real and the truth of the idyllic vision of expanding Hrothgar's kingdom, as expressed by the Shaper.

The rhetoric of the narrative, with its particulars of description and detail of the horrors, in combination with Grendel's knowledge that his emotional reaction to the art, directly contrasts the truth as he has witnessed it, as well as the logical paradox presented by the dual truths, prompts one to accept his perspective as valid. After hearing the Shaper, Grendel states: "I knew the truth . . . I remembered the ragged men fighting each other till the snow was red slush . . . Yet I also remembered, as if it had happened, great Scyld, of whose kingdom no trace remained . . . And the stars overhead were alive with the promise of Hrothgar's vast power, his universal peace" (44).

If Grendel's observations are correct, and we have no reason to believe he has misinterpreted man's bloody acts, then the Shaper has created a convenient lie "for a price." There is nothing virtuous in doing so, it does not appear to be an act of deliverance for humans, nor does it correspond to any of Gardner's descriptions of moral art. Grendel feels torn by the discrepancy between the truth as he has seen it (and convincingly conveyed it) and the heroic and lofty twists put upon it by the Shaper's art: "Thus I fled, ridiculous hairy creature torn apart by poetry— crawling, whimpering, streaming tears, across the world like a two-headed beast, like a mixed-up lamb and kid at the tail of a baffled, indifferent ewe—and I gnashed my teeth and clutched the sides of my head as if to heal the split, but I couldn't" (44).

The image of twin-ness in this passage and in the paragraph above it "Every sheep and goat had its wobbly twins" (44) emphasizes the split. Similarly, the image as it applies to Grendel is worth noting. For Grendel, the rhetorical pairing of the lamb and the goat emphasizes the contrast between them, one with significant symbolic differences. As well, note the reference to his mother, as a "baffled ewe." Grendel as progeny is "a two-headed beast . . . a mixed-up lamb and kid."

Traditionally, the lamb stands for the innocence of unblemished sacrifice (often extended to a Christ symbol), whereas the goat or the "kid" connotes rebellion and Devil symbolism. It could be surmised that here, at least, the connection between Cain and the Devil means that Grendel's (human) paternal side connects him to evil. At this point in the novel, the Shaper has not discussed the Cain and Abel story, so the reference to Grendel's paternal roots would not be specific; still, his search for identity finds no outlet in his mother ("baffled and indifferent"), so it would make sense for him to search the male lineage for answers, just as in Chapter Two his references to the others in the cave were male, "uncles" or "brothers" not "aunts" and "sisters."

Other dualities are present as well. His mother is a natural creature without language or art and seemingly content with her existence, while Grendel feels tortured by his lack of identity and community, or even an audience. Grendel, who has not attacked Hrothgar's court and remains unknown to the thanes except as a possible creature who haunts the moors, nonetheless senses in his outcast state a lack of grace, a split between himself and the proper world—concretized by the Shaper's poem—which has outcast him. Similarly, his "murderous unrest" begins to take shape in response to the Shaper's art and his own growing need for identity.

In effect, the Shaper provides a paradigm, the power of his art inspiring the humans with notions of their own greatness, whereas Grendel seeks acknowledgement of his own existence and his place in the world. At the chapter's end, Grendel shrieks twice and both contain significant markers of his search for identity. In the first shriek, in apparent anger at the division between truth and art, the sound goes out to the "rims of the world," and then echoes " . . . harsh and ungodly against the sigh of the remembered harp—like a thousand tortured rat-squeals crying," mirroring the description of humans as rat-like in Chapter Two. This tells us how Grendel sees himself, the human side of him feeling torment, as well as his prescience of himself as attacker and tormenter.

Of the second shriek, Grendel says, "I clamped my palms to my ears and stretched up my lips and shrieked again: a stab at truth, a snatch at apocalyptic glee" (45), an interesting choice of words seeming, again, to foreshadow disruption and demise, first of Hrothgar's glorious court, and then of Grendel himself. Here, Grendel attempts to displace the Shaper's false truth with his own, and we see the beginnings of his putting such feelings into action. The chapter ends with the statement, "Then I ran on all fours, chest pounding, to the smoky mere," (45) showing us Grendel as animal again, headed back to his own den, where he feels most safe.

It has become increasingly clear, however, that Grendel's search for identity cannot have as its result a mere return to the natural state; Grendel, because of his self-consciousness and the need to communicate, must have some type of interaction with intelligent others. If he cannot find contentment (such as his mother seems to feel) in the cave-dwelling isolated state, then it stands to reason he will search for another way to have an audience.

John Gardner and Existentialism

Extended outward, some scholars see the novel as a lesson against existentialism, suggesting that Grendel's view of life is false, causing him to grow evil. The humor, therefore, would be in each of us having a bit of the existentialist in us, and sometimes then becoming the loathsome monster, seeing the human community as ridiculous and hypocritical when, this position would assert, it is not so. The problems here are twofold, first as concerns Gardner's views on existentialism and second the implication of the untrustworthy narrator.

In Marshall L. Harvey's 1977 interview, Gardner says: "Sartre is my great love-hate . . . I got the idea of presenting the *Beowulf* monster as Jean-Paul Sartre, and everything that Grendel says Sartre in one mood or another has said, so that my love of Sartre kind of comes through as my love of the monster, though monsters are still monsters, I hope."[32] Here, he shows his affection for both Sartre and Grendel, but one must be careful not to assume that Grendel is being misleading in his recounting of events simply because he holds existentialist ideas.

Rather than reading "Grendel as Sartre" as a way of Gardner's repudiation of Sartre (by having existentialist theories spouted by a monster), one may see Gardner constructing a larger experiment. In Gardner's 1978 interview with Heide Ziegler, his discussion of existentialism would seem to support such a reading, " . . . it was only when the French underground was living an impossible life in which the odds were overwhelmingly against it that suddenly existentialism came in as a persuasive philosophy . . . It's a wonderful theory—if you are a French existentialist in the underground, where because of history's momentum—the odds—you haven't got a chance. If you believe, you die happy."[33]

Gardner's Grendel, of course, doesn't have a chance. He attempts to reinvent himself time and again, to claim an identity separate from his fate, one which, as readers of the poem, we know he cannot escape. In Grendel's situation, the "wonderful theory" of existentialism allows him to believe he has a chance at happiness. If it is in fact Grendel's desperate isolation that leads him to existentialism, this shifts the inquiry from the choice itself to the underpinning angst.

In Chapter Two, where the novel goes back in time to recount the beginning of Grendel's relationship with humans, one is hard-pressed to see the accounts of humans as false, or his description of his own innocence as false. If we accept his recounting of events as basically trustworthy, if we have no reason to see his childhood innocence as false, then the moral center of the novel reflects the tragedy of distorted self-awareness, as seen in both Grendel and his human counterparts.

It does not, however, propose what some Gardner scholars have maintained in their attempts to ally the themes of the book with *On Moral Fiction*: it does not sidestep Grendel's view and instead laud the true morality of one or more of the humans, such as the Shaper, Unferth, Hrothgar, or even Beowulf himself (which I will discuss as we come to chapters in the novel highlighting those characters). There is no need for such a shift, because a novel reflecting the tragedy of social alienation and distorted self-awareness is likely, by its nature, to be moral and life

---

[32] Marshall L. Harvey, "Where Philosophy and Fiction Meet, an Interview with John Gardner," in *Conversations with John Gardner*, edited Allan Chavkin (University of Mississippi Press, 1990), 86-98

[33] Heide Ziegler, "John Gardner," in *Conversations with John Gardner*, edited Allan Chavkin (University of Mississippi Press, 1990), 117-142

affirming, even if it does not seem so. Most modern and postmodern novels where conflicts are psychological (as Howell sees *Grendel*), even when they are ironically humorous, have their basis in truth.

Gardner, in several interviews, classifies *Beowulf's* Grendel as symbolic of the "rational soul gone perverse."[34] He notes that the moment of inspiration for his novel was the recognition of such a symbol being fully functional in the modern world, as seen in existentialism. I'm suggesting that Grendel's perversity in the novel comes from the disparity between egoism and one's need to submit the ego—or, self-awareness distorted by a perverse rationale. I make this distinction because the humans within the novel are consistently wedded to more traditional ways of seeing life, yet they are equally unhappy and unsuccessful. So, while existentialism or Nietzsche's notion of the superman or any number of other philosophies may blind one's ability to perceive the self, so too may notions of nationalism, heroism, and religion, to name a few. Gardner need not privilege Grendel's outlook over the humans or vice versa.

Still, in *On Moral Fiction*, he points to the debate between Plato and Aristotle concerning whether a poet's showing a "good man performing a bad act" is immoral art. While Plato held such art to be immoral, Aristotle corrected him, and Gardner asserts, "It's the total effect of an action that's moral or immoral bad . . . it's the energeia (the actualization of the potential which exists in character and situation) that gives us the poet's fix on good and evil; that is, dramatically demonstrates the moral laws, and the possibility of tragic waste, in the universe. . ."[35]

Many of Gardner's novels, *October Light* and *The Sunlight Dialogues* come to mind, have conflicts in which opposing views, when taken to the extreme, are equally false. Likewise, in nearly all his works, as scholars point out, individuals are protected from their own misguided views by the power of community, either active or symbolic: what dooms one to tragedy is the isolation from society. It is no different in *Grendel*. What better way to explore these themes than with a doomed but magnificent monster?

As well, this would explain why Gardner creates a monster with endearing qualities, encouraging us by the first-person perspective to take part in its pain, and showing the creature's initial personality as innocent. Otherwise, the novel becomes a lesson against deceit, not simply on levels of self-awareness (for Grendel deceives himself constantly just as he is deceived by others—and the humans do the same) but between writer and

---

[34] Ed Christian, "An Interview with John Gardner" in *Conversations with John Gardner*, edited Allan Chavkin (University of Mississippi Press, 1990), 193

[35] (Gardner, *On Moral Fiction*, 23)

reader, with Gardner as moralist preaching against the reader's natural inclination to believe the protagonist and engage with his struggles.

Such a stance would seem contrary to everything Gardner claims to be important about what he sees as the true artist, in *On Moral Fiction*, but many other places as well, including interviews, formal and informal, *On Becoming a Novelist*, and *The Art of Fiction*. The subject arises in an interview with Ed Christian, who observes, "In your book *On Moral Fiction* you write that the great writer must have a settled system of moral belief . . . " He goes on, " . . . and must feel a love for his characters, must empathize with them, whether they are good or bad . . . Your later books radiate much more care for an involvement with your characters than your early books do."

Gardner responds, "I think you underestimate my early books. I think the early books are deeply moral. They're always on the same moral subject. Faith versus rationality is what I always talk about. Grendel is, from beginning to end, a character distrusting faith." Christian then says, "When one reads a book, one can tell, just by the way the author writes about his characters, whether he really cares for them or not," and Gardner responds, "It's obvious in *Grendel*. Anybody can see that. Everybody falls in love with the monster."[36]

Few "fall in love" with the monsters as they are presented in *Beowulf*, creatures separated from grace through an inherited curse. Even so, and for all of their violent deeds, Grendel and his mother are portrayed at times with sympathy on the part of the *Beowulf* poet: the emphasis on Grendel's "endurance of hardship" as he hears the "loud mirth" of the hall, in the context of his isolated state; his mother's pain which is immediately paired with the idea of her living place, "Grendel's mother, woman, monster-wife, was mindful of her misery, she who had to dwell in the terrible water, the cold currents, after Cain became sword-slayer of his only brother," and she goes on a "sorrowful venture" to "avenge her son's death."[37]

The lack of grace separates them from God and man, yet even in 1000 A.D. the outcast state creates empathy, as the poet puts some focus on their desolation where he or she may have instead limited the descriptions to vileness. I don't mean to belie the hellish qualities of Grendel and his mother in the poem, nor to offer a reading radically different from the most accepted; however, it is nonetheless true that the horror of Grendel and his dam comes not from their dissimilarity from humans, but from

---

[36] (Christian "Interview with John Gardner," 198-199)
[37] (Donaldson, *trans., Beowulf*, 23)

their very humanness[38]—they are not alien beasts even to the extent that the dragon is an alien beast—they are creatures who feel human emotions and react in human ways.

Their disrespect for human rules and boundaries, juxtaposed with their human connection, creates a distinctly high form of horror, just as we are revolted by the notion of cannibalism while merely aghast at the notion of wild animals eating humans. I see Gardner recognizing in the poem an opportunity to explore the ideas of the ultimate human outcast—one so far outcast as to have outgrown a conscious allegiance to humanity while at the same time maintaining vital conscious and subconscious associations. There is irony here, to be sure, and paradox as well, but while these function as part of alterity when it comes to characters in literature, the point of alterity for most traditional (by this, I mean "not postmodern") artists is in reader identification, not in reader disassociation.

This concerns the values Gardner explores in the work. If Grendel is strictly ironic, then his reasons for being violent, such as existentialism, are by extension a potentially monstrous philosophy in humans—Grendel says what Sartre says and both are misguided and unhappy, as well as unproductive to humanity (or so it may seem). While no doubt true in some respects (Gardner himself has said what amounts to this), it does limit his novel to such a truncated view.

Recasting Grendel as the protagonist-existentialist monster begs the question of how he came to be this way. This is not purely the result of Grendel's unfortunate attraction to a misguided philosophy, though this exists in the novel. It is as well, and more importantly, the consequence of the errors of the human community, similar to the monster in *Frankenstein*, for which, as Howell points out, Gardner wrote a libretto.[39]

The root cause of Grendel's misperceptions, which lead to his existentialism and self-centeredness, is not his own lack of humanity, nor a lack of exposure to human art and society and nation-building, which Gardner takes great pains to show, but humanity's lack of compassion for him. The lesson here is not to avoid being Grendel but to point out exactly how we ourselves create our Grendels—and how, at every opportunity to redeem them, we further isolate them. Grendel is to blame as well, of course, yet the onus of a society which claims to be civilized is in its ability to resolve problems without violence.

No such stipulations were placed on Anglo-Saxon society, which emphasized the importance of a king's ability to provide stability (by

---

[38] Again, see Tolkien's "*Beowulf*: The Monsters & the Critics"

[39] (Howell, *Understanding John Gardner*, 70)

knocking over the mead hall benches of other kings) and to reward his followers for helping him do so, which somehow was in accordance with God's grace. But a Western civilization that claims democracy as its primary value necessarily promotes the importance of the individual. Inclusion in society, therefore, becomes important, lest the republic fall into a chaos of individual needs. The outcast, then, becomes a test for the morality of any social system.

This conflict between the power structures of society and the outcast functions in nearly every one of Gardner's works. At times, the character's physical deformities or differences separate him from society, such as Freddy the giant (*Freddy's Book*) and the less large but equally outcast Henry Soames (*Nickel Mountain*). In some cases, including the Sunlight Man (*The Sunlight Dialogues*), insanity creates physical repulsion in onlookers. In others, Gardner's characters who would appear to be accepted, whom members of the society take pains to try and include, outcast themselves because of a distaste for social hypocrisies, characters like Fred Clumly (*The Sunlight Dialogues*), James Abbott (*October Light*) and Pete Mickelsson (*Mickelsson's Ghosts*). Indeed, one is hard-pressed to find a Gardner work without such a conflict. *Grendel* is no different.

Gardner Scholars, the Shaper, and *On Moral Fiction*

Several scholars of Gardner's works, those whose arguments are sound as applied to all of them except *Grendel*, sometimes struggle to find a place for it among the other novels. Specifically, on the topic of good versus evil, they lock themselves into elevating the moral stature of characters whom Grendel has convincingly portrayed as idiotic and hypocritical. Complicating the matter, such an elevation would seem to correspond (they say) to Gardner's theories on the ethics of art. The answer to "How can this novel be considered 'life affirming' since the protagonist is a bloodthirsty maniac?" becomes something like, "Because the real hero is [fill in the blank]," along with the occasional side comment that Gardner meant the novel as a joke, a condemnation of Anglo-Saxon life, or simply as a dark parody.

David Cowart sees the novel's real central conflict as being between the Shaper and Grendel, both characters who are creators of art, with the Shaper winning in the end because his art is more uplifting while Grendel's is destructive.[40] The argument is alluring because it answers the novel's seeming incongruous stance with Gardner's theories on art and

---

[40] (Cowart, *Arches & Light*, 38)

morality, thus as Cowart puts it, the Shaper is representative of "good (art)," and Grendel as "bad (art)": "Thus the battle between Grendel and Beowulf, a contest of strength, takes second place in importance to the indirect competition between Grendel and the Shaper—a contest of art. The story ultimately concerns the triumph of good art over bad, for in it Grendel manages only self-indictment. He unwittingly produces a case history of the bad artist, as John Gardner would define such a monster." Cowart seems not to acknowledge that Grendel portrays the Shaper as an opportunist of the highest sort—supremely talented, talented enough to fool the humans into thinking themselves godlike—but nonetheless a man focused on reward of a material sort.

Ronald Nutter agrees with Cowart's argument, but says, "Grendel . . . cannot fully accept the old man's vision in spite of its attraction, for Grendel is a self-proclaimed truth teller who will not let go of what he knows to be a more accurate depiction of the human: a murderer capable of the most self-serving and vicious acts in a manifestly absurd world."[41] Nutter is right in this, for Gardner gives us no indication that Grendel has misinterpreted the humans. With the exception of a few characters such as Ork and Wealtheow, mankind is reprehensible.

This is not to say Gardner finds the Shaper's art to be unhealthy for mankind. Indeed, it may serve a useful (though twisted) purpose, but it would be difficult to accept the Shaper as Gardner's ideal symbol of virtue, artistic or otherwise. Nor can one maintain Cowart's allegorical view of the Shaper as virtuous by separating artistic virtue from actual virtue, for Gardner is absolutely clear in this regard, as stated in *On Moral Fiction,* "True art is by its nature moral. We recognize true art by its careful, thoroughly honest search for and analysis of values."[42] Of the Shaper himself Gardner has stated, " . . . he tells the truth, although he lies."[43]

Nutter's examination of the novel recognizes the paradox, yet he maintains the value of the Shaper's vision and in its contribution to the community. While many readers will feel the need to choose between the Shaper's vision and Grendel's, Nutter says, those who know Gardner's work will admit Grendel's role as destroyer of mankind. The novel, he maintains, is " . . . a statement of the worth of human life, as envisioned and projected in the art of a culture, and emulated in the lives of men and women in a community."[44] Further, Nutter suggests, difficulty in finding

[41] (Nutter, *A Dream of Peace: Art and Death in the Fiction of John Gardner*, 66)

[42] (Gardner, *On Moral Fiction*, 19)

[43] (Bellamy, "John Gardner,"15)

[44] (Nutter, *A Dream of Peace*, 74)

evidence of such emulation of culture, community, or some combination thereof, may be explained by Grendel's prejudiced view.

As do Cowart, Nutter, and Butts, Gregory Morris sees the Shaper as positive, " . . . he transmutes the past like an alchemist, mixing truth with lie until a vision emerges, a vision that annihilates pain and exalts human effort."[45] However, nowhere in *On Moral Fiction* (or Gardner's other books on theory) is such a "mixing of truth with lie" advocated, nor even permitted. Gardner asserts, " . . . there can be no moral social art (as Doctorow's errors show) without honesty in the individual— the artist—as a premise for just and reasonable discussion,"[46] and "An artist is someone who believes . . . that art reflects something which is real in life . . . If he panders to his time, saying what his time says no matter how his art cries out against him, he is a witch, and dangerous."[47] The Shaper most certainly panders to his time, and to Hrothgar's vanity in particular.

Some scholars argue that the Shaper's art serves a constructive purpose by providing a sense of unity. Morris has cited Joe Bellamy's interview with Gardner and said it is clear Gardner means for us to see the Shaper's art as "virtuous" (59). Yet an examination of the context may show otherwise. Pat Ensworth, one of the interviewers, makes this observation, "Shelley's view of the poet seems to be in conflict with the role you present in *Grendel*. The Shaper incites his community to war; Grendel sees him as a liar and a destructive force."[48] Gardner's response (the one cited by Morris) is as follows, "The Shaper comes along in a meaningless, stupid kingdom and makes up a rationale. He creates the heroism, the feeling of tribal unity. He makes the people brave. And sure, it's a lie, but it's also a vision" (as also qtd. in Morris, 59).

Gardner is not promoting the Shaper's art as "virtuous" but merely explaining the Shaper as an artist of opportunity—not a "destructive force" to mankind, necessarily, except in the larger view, in Grendel's view. Now, the question comes again in how one is to take Grendel's view, whether he is seen as an outsider who cannot understand humans and so draws false conclusions about them, or whether he is one whose outcast state gives him a wider and clearer perspective on man's role in the world.

In other words, the Shaper's art may serve to make a corrupt society a more functional corrupt society, and even to make the people feel better about their lives, but I would argue with Morris that this does not make it moral, virtuous, or even "good." Indeed, the very fact of it being a lie

---

[45] (Morris, A World of Order and Light, 58)
[46] (Gardner, On Moral Fiction, 82)
[47] (Gardner, On Moral Fiction, 169)
[48] (Bellamy, "John Gardner," 15)

discounts such definitions. During the same interview, what must have been only a few moments before, for instance, to Bellamy's question of what Gardner saw as the "writer's responsibility to perpetuate only . . . 'positive' moral values" (13), Gardner responded, "The ultimate moral value, the moral value I really look for beyond anything else, is to be exactly truthful—seeing things clearly, the process of art. Art is the absolute morality because the good artist won't go to the next sentence until this sentence is perfect and says what's true." The Shaper, therefore, cannot be said to be a moral artist.

In a vein similar to Morris', Cowart claims the Shaper "changes men, and for the better," and is the good artist, "our true deliverer," in contrast to Grendel, who "lacks the power of a transforming imagination . . . and changes nothing."[49] Several questions arise. First, is there any proof of the Shaper changing mankind for the better? Hrothgar grows stronger and more powerful, but not necessarily better. Secondly, since the Shaper arrives before Grendel has started to attack, from what or whom does the Shaper deliver mankind? An argument might be made for the Shaper as an essential element in mankind's demise, as Pat Ensworth seems to have suggested in the Bellamy interview. Lastly, is it fair to characterize Grendel's imagination as lacking power when in fact he has neither artistic outlet nor wider human audience? One is tempted to argue for the novel itself as representative of Grendel's imaginative power, given its first-person narration, and to suggest it lacks neither creativity nor power.

As noted, the desire to divide the novel along lines of good and evil comes from its peculiarity amongst Gardner's novels, principally a narrator at odds with all of humanity. However, to see Gardner as championing the human characters is to call into question the entire perspective (and relative value) in Grendel's standpoints. This is not borne out in the prose, in my opinion. The problem in such an approach comes from Grendel's explicit descriptions of the vileness with which men treat one another before the Shaper's arrival—and there is no reason to believe he is lying or even exaggerating these descriptions—combined with his clear view of the Shaper as bolstering, even encouraging, the human community's desire for bloodshed.

The prose is clear in this respect. Only through completely discounting Grendel's observations, and then judging the brutality and aggressiveness of Hrothgar's attacks as somehow necessary, may one could see the Shaper's art as ultimately or even partially positive. Although the Shaper's art occasionally has a gentling effect on the humans, the worth of it to the

---

[49] (Cowart, *Arches & Light*, 40-41)

community is complicated, because it also incites them to murder. In how many better ways might a true moral artist have affected the Hrothgar's Danes?

If one could imagine, for instance, Chapter Two's encounter with men turning out differently, wherein the idea of Grendel as a "tree spirit" (25) led to their seeing him as a type of natural deity, or if the humans had been better able to understand Grendel's speech (as, later, Unferth is), he may well have been able to inspire them toward a more peaceful existence, a more natural way of life. Failing at that, he may even have joined them as their new and most powerful warrior.

One may respond that the parameters of the original tale preclude such a conversion, yet my point is to show how Gardner establishes truly positive aspects of Grendel's personality, ones that remain unappreciated or unseen by the humans in the novel. Nor is Gardner averse to challenging the parameters of the poem, so long as the basic facts of the story remain in place. Consider the following statements made by Gardner in a 1977 interview with Charlie Reilly, which branched off from a discussion about Gardner's epic poem *Jason and Medeia*: " . . . a practice developed, one which is directly linked to what we're discussing in my *Jason and Medeia*, which involved using translation in the formation of poems. In this case, the wish was to preserve the spirit of the original but to apply it to completely different political situations and so on . . . Chaucer changed lines around and made a number of creative decisions which totally transmogrify the poem.[50] I attempted . . . the use of a Chaucerian method. I don't mean to imply I created a better work that *Apollonius' Argonautica*— or that my *Grendel* is in any way an improvement on *Beowulf*."[51]

If *Grendel* is, indeed, a transmogrification of *Beowulf*, with the spirit of the original applied to "completely different political situations," then the outcast creature voicing his anger and distrust with the war state works. For Gardner to keep the poem's essentials intact, the creature must at some point lose control and become truly evil, yet in going back to an earlier point in Grendel's history, Gardner cleverly shows the inspiration for such vileness to have been the aggression found in society; Grendel sees himself as providing retribution on a society which, itself, lauds the conqueror.

To misread this and see the humans as praiseworthy is to miscalculate the entire moral fabric of the novel. Further, to suggest Gardner means

---

[50] Gardner is discussing Chaucer's translation of Boccaccio's poem

[51] Charlie Reilly, "A Conversation with John Gardner," *Conversations with John Gardner*, edited Allan Chavkin (University of Mississippi Press, 1990), 66

only to critique the aggression of Anglo-Saxon society and not modern American society would seem to ignore Gardner's own statements concerning translations, to "preserve the spirit of the original but to apply it to completely different political situations."

CHAPTER TWO

BATTLE ONE: ENTER A STRANGER

Gardner's Scholarship on Ideologies in *Beowulf*

For Gardner, the poem is a Christian allegory containing various symbols. Within this, it uses "pagan material for a Christian purpose." Of the allegorical styles, Gardner lists three types: linear, vertical, and circular. He states, "The linear style helps to shape the poem through echoes and repetitions" such as "parallel passages," which become aligned by logic in the reader's imagination. The second type, vertical, Gardner sees in " . . . the poet's handling of the mead hall image, his three monsters, and other elements," or, in other words, the use of encoded symbols and metaphors which simultaneously represent multiple ideas and characters (54-55). When Grendel attacks but cannot "occupy" the mead hall, it reflects his lack of grace with God, Hrothgar's lack of grace with God, the mead hall as a metaphor of the body (so it may be seen as a body without a head, reflected as well in Grendel's decapitation of thanes), the coming apocalypse of man with the central mead hall overtaken by a thane from Hell, and so on (62-63).

In *Beowulf*, Gardner explains, the poet uses circular allegory in combination with lingual tensions, through which, "Allegorical overtones intensify the irony . . . This mystical rather than logical or metaphoric form of allegory appears at various points in *Beowulf*. But there is a major difference between the *Beowulf*-poet's use of this 'circular' allegory and Cynewulf's use of the same thing. In *Beowulf*, it is supportive, not central: it provides lyrical climaxes (some of the finest moments in the poem), it pushes the listener beyond thought to religious and aesthetic ecstasy; but because it is only one stylistic element among many in the poem, it does not suggest abnegation of thought for mystical release, escape from reality for pure celebration" (117).

The question becomes, how then does allegory function in Gardner's novel? Under scrutiny, as I have treated them, each chapter uses metaphors of all three types, linear and vertical as well as the more ironic circular (mystical) motifs. Within this, Gardner weaves into Grendel's stream of consciousness various characters and situations from previous episodes. Per Winther, in his study *The Art of John Gardner*, notes that while Morris, Butts, and Cowart investigate the influence of Gardner's philosophies on his fiction, more scholarship is needed in the area of his literary techniques. Winther focuses on those talents which set Gardner apart from (and above) his literary peers: his highly developed narrative voice and his technique of alluding to past literary tradition. Winther has termed the combination of voice and allusion his "collage technique," which he explains as Gardner's attempt to "explore and communicate whatever 'truths' he arrives at in his writing."[52]

As well, one can see how the Fulgentian scheme, which Gardner saw as the unifying nucleus of the poem in its use of the tripartite soul,[53] links the two works, particularly in relation to the three-battle sequence and Grendel as hero. Gardner's own analysis of *Beowulf* is extensive, found primarily in *The Construction of Christian Poetry in Old English*, though his other works in medieval studies also shed light on his theories, including his books *The Complete Works of the Gawain Poet*, *The Life and Times of Chaucer*, and *The Construction of the Wakefield Cycle.*

In terms of the allegorical framework of the poem, Gardner expands upon previous scholarly work by Kaske, Leyerle and others, on the connection between the structure of the three battles in Beowulf and Fulgentius' arma, virum, and primus, suggesting this scheme as one of the keys to interpreting its allegorical framework.[54] The parallels are complex, for there is the related matter of man's tripartite soul (rational, irascible, and concupiscent). They suggest a one-to-one correspondence between the character development of Beowulf the hero and the poem's three battles.

Gardner suggests each stage may be seen in both a positive and a negative light within and between the battles. For instance, arma (the action and might of weapons and human strength) dictates Scyld's rise to

---

[52] Per Winther, *The Art of John Gardner* (Albany: SUNY Press, 1982), 7. Winther sees his strengths in the dialectical method, the "juxtaposing contrary ideas and principles (such as order and disorder, body and mind), watching closely to see what truths may issue from the ideational conflict." Further, for Winther, Grendel's lack of belief in consistent patterns within the universe is contradicted within Gardner's ordering of the novel around the zodiac cycle—Gardner's assertion, according to Winther, of Grendel's mistaken perceptions, because the monster, too, is affected by and exists within this cycle (173).

[53] (Gardner, *The Construction of Christian Poetry in Old English*, 55)

[54] (Gardner, *The Construction of Christian Poetry in Old English*, 55-57)

power as well as Hrothgar's, and may be seen in Beowulf's journeying to Hrothgar's court to battle Grendel. God rewards arma if it is valorous: princes such as Hrothgar and Beowulf rise to power from the starting point of their action and might of arms. Even Scyld, according to Gardner, represents such arma because he ascends to power via the workings of good leadership (though as Dr. Christopher Cain points out, Scyld is distinct from the other two because of his mysterious origins and his arrival as an infant in the treasure-laden ship).[55] However, Gardner goes so far as to see Grendel himself as reflecting a type of arma, an "arma gone mad."[56]

Virum relates to wisdom and loyalty, what might be called the tempering of action with reason. Brave deeds in and of themselves are fine, but when they become part of a just system, they develop into the kingly code of behavior. This code, one which Scyld, Hrothgar, and Beowulf all adhere to, (a repeated phrase in the poem, "baet waes god cyning!"[57]), reflects fealty and community. Again, the inversion of this may be seen, Gardner suggests, in the second battle of the poem.[58] Grendel's mother attacks due to her unfortunate loyalty to her dead son (unfortunate because all of them are cursed as offspring of Cain), and so her virum comes not from wisdom but as a result of vengeful retribution; this, Gardner asserts, explains why the poet chose as her victim Aeschere, Hrothgar's most loyal and beloved retainer, a symbol of positive Danish virum. Moreover, Beowulf, in choosing to fight her, becomes an accepted part of the Danes' community, as symbolized by Unferth's giving him Hrunting, the heirloom sword (70).

Primus, according to Gardner's interpretation of Fulgentius, corresponds to wealth, fame, security, earthly possessions and position. Beowulf's position as he enters his battle with the dragon is one of respected kingship. His kingdom is threatened and he prepares to defend it, a conflict touched off by the servant stealing from the dragon's hoard. The dragon represents primus gone bad, the avaricious hoarding of treasures and the madness resulting from it.

Note, however, that for Gardner, the three Fulgentian ideals correspond fluidly to the characters and battles, rather than being essences like wisdom which are increased with age: Gardner sees Beowulf at the stage of primus as lacking in virum, a result of having become too focused on

---

55 Christopher Cain, notes on "Grendel as Allegory," submitted by Sandra Hiortdahl, The Catholic University of America (2006)

56 (Gardner, *The Construction of Christian Poetry in Old English*, 69)

57 Translated, "That was a good king!"

58 (Gardner, *The Construction of Christian Poetry in Old English*, 70)

power (as represented by the treasure) and not focused enough on "community," which would have allowed him to recognize the need for more loyal retainers in order to survive the battle with the dragon (70).

For Gardner, the most virtuous of characters suffer from failings of virtue, and the monsters themselves are illustrations of virtue gone wrong, suggesting virtue once present. One may argue, for instance, in Grendel's mother having no choice with respect to virtue: her loyalty to her son cannot be virtuous because of God's decree, yet disloyalty would be equally lacking in virtue; her inherited misalliances preclude her ability to attain virtue. Clearly, if his approach to the poem allows virtue to be extended and transmuted, as well as reversed even for the "best" of characters, then his own novel could contain such fluidity.

This is not to say Gardner saw the idea of form as dispensable. He states in *The Forms of Fiction,* " . . . form is the meaningful organization and arrangement of various elements in a work . . . Form, in other words, is not something all fiction has but something a good work of fiction achieves. A work becomes a good work, or achieves form, when all of its elements are functionally and proportionally related to one another."[59] For Gardner, the form of *Beowulf* as an allegory need not be compromised by a more flexible approach to virtue: i.e., a hero's actions can be a reflection of either positive or negative virtues, given the situation.

Similarly, a monster such as Grendel's mother can display actions of loyalty which are perverted not by any inner depravity but by her state as one condemned by God. Since Gardner views the poem as having complexity of form and a variety of influences, and since he equates good fiction with "functional and proportional elements," one would expect his retelling of *Beowulf* from the monster's point of view to be complex as well as highly structured.

Grendel, Chapter Four, Surveying the Text

Chapter Four opens with Grendel returning the narrative to the present moment, the end of his twelve years of terror, and he begins here to explain the real power of the Shaper to change the course of events, in creating the mead hall which would become Grendel's focal point for attack: "He built this hall by the power of his songs: created with casual words its grave mor(t)ality" (47). As Grendel sees it, the Shaper has inspired the building, with its "morality" a supposed validation of human

---

[59] John Gardner, and Lennis Dunlap, *eds.*, *The Forms of Fiction, an Anthology* (New York: Random House, 1962)

endeavor transformed via pun to "mortality," the deaths which result from the enraged monster's attacks. Nor is the building of the mead hall a mere suggestion to Hrothgar on the poet's part: Grendel suggests that the poetic force itself creates the idea and sets the construction in motion.

Significant parallels connect Grendel's emotional aspects to these actions. The Shaper "sang of a glorious mead hall whose light would shine to the ends of the ragged world" (47). Note the echoes with the end of the last chapter as Grendel's first scream goes to the "rims of the world" (45). There, Grendel's "chest pounded" (45), while here he states, "My heart was light with Hrothgar's goodness, and leaden with guilt at my own bloodthirsty ways" (48). At this point, it seems important not to misinterpret this self-description as an indication Grendel has started his systematic attacks, for both the chapter as it continues and the structure of the poem propose the episode of the first attack be at the *new mead hall*, Heorot (or Hart), that in this chapter the Shaper is suggesting, perhaps forseeing.

The term "bloodthirsty ways" refers to Shaper's song that has described the race cursed by God. Grendel, having been unable to define an identity for himself, hears for the first time of the divisions between good and evil, knows he is not one of the humans who have been blessed, and so adopts the only role left to him. One can see how the Shaper inspires not only the mead hall itself, but the very creature who will make it infamous. Despite the glory in the scop's song, Grendel's logic prevents him from accepting this vision of Hrothgar's goodness. He remembers with meticulous detail the blood and gore he has seen. Despite his disgust, he has felt fascination with the horror, causing him to doggedly follow their exploits.

The humans may be vulgar and murderous, but they are the only creatures to whom Grendel can connect. However, their penchant for masking their violence with self-deceptive songs of glory mystifies him. As the chapter continues, Grendel reveals the sense of guilt carried with him since childhood, an acknowledgement of his separation from the humans. The image of a crab, symbolic of Cancer (the astrological sign following Gemini and the fourth in the zodiac cycle, corresponding to the chapter's number) functions prominently as an associative metaphor.

The chapter started from the narrative present, where we left off in Chapter One, a cynical Grendel near the end of his destructions who watches the funeral pyre burn. Here, the crab image links the natural world to the emotional upheavals wrought by the monster's rages, "The sun backs away like a crab and the days grow shorter, the nights grow longer, more dark and dangerous. I smile, angry in the thickening dusk, and feast my eyes on the greatest of mead halls, unsatisfied" (46).

The pyre has consumed the body, just as the fire of the sun has lessened because it, too, has gone. Even as the darkness comes, Grendel then applies the image of fire to the mead hall itself, foreshadowing the fire with which Heorot eventually will be consumed, though this knowledge is unavailable to Grendel, who will die long before it occurs. In thus shifting between the irascible anger of the destroyer and the relative innocence of adolescence, Gardner emphasizes the contrast, heightening the reader's desire to know more completely how such a turnabout came to be. The image of the crab, which itself represents a variety of emotional markers, connects these pieces; as well, it combines with symbolic elements of heat and cold, light and darkness, as the crab itself is an emotional reactor to these states, just as, in the opening, it represented the "retreating" sun.

As Grendel, back in the past, listens to the Shaper changing and ultimately distorting man's self-image, the creature himself becomes the crab, and his darkness an emotional one: "I listened, felt myself swept up. I knew very well that all he said was ridiculous, not light for their darkness but flattery, illusion, a vortex pulling them from sunlight to heat . . . I backed away, crablike, further into darkness—like a crab retreating in pain when you strike two stones at the mouth of his underwater den." From Grendel's perspective, the onus of his behavior is on the humans and their hypocrisy. The Shaper's songs, in contradicting the violent human acts and Grendel's perception of men as evil, create a completely convincing false reality. Grendel, in knowing his own memories to be true, nonetheless feels guilt at not adopting the "new reality."

Just as the sun was crablike in the opening, Grendel becomes crablike at this point in the narrative. The disparity in the two situations heightens the contrast between past and present, for in the present Grendel's murderous attacks on the mead hall cause pain, while in the past his own pain comes from guilt and confusion over the Shaper's songs. Having retreated from the harp's sounds, Grendel struggles to make sense of the situation. The Shaper has changed the world with his words whereas Grendel's own talking to himself amounts to " . . . eternal posturing . . . changing nothing" (49). Inklings of a supernatural connection between art and a force beyond occur to Grendel, for the Shaper plucks his strings " . . . as if moved by something beyond his power" (49).

Simultaneously, a certain unseen presence felt by Grendel begins to make itself more known, one symbolically connected to snakes, cold, and death. The split so far highlighted in the chapter, between the comfort of light/heat and the threat of dark/cold makes a leap from characters and character reactions to a level beyond known reality. This occurs just as Grendel recognizes the sublimity of art in conjunction with his own feelings of guilt and powerlessness. The scene is thus set for an epiphany. Grendel enters a clearing, aware of the human adolescents who have paired up in the darkness outside of the mead hall. There, he stumbles upon a human corpse with its throat cut and its clothes stolen, epitome of mankind's malevolence, and is stunned by the discrepancies between the evidence of evil and the oblivious innocence of the human teenagers.

As he lifts the corpse and puts it over his shoulder, the Shaper begins to sing "as sweet-voiced as a child" (51). The song echoes the section of *Beowulf* that prefigures the monster's attack, a description fronted by the lines of *Beowulf* the poem, "Then the fierce spirit painfully endured hardship for a time, he who dwelt in the darkness, for every day he heard loud mirth in the hall; there was the sound of the harp, the clear song of the scop."[60] According to Gardner's novel, this "endured hardship" comes not as a response to isolation from the human's unity and glee, but in recognition of their actual wickedness, so that the Shaper's song reflects the ultimate hypocrisy, while at the same time casting Grendel in the role of outsider, the races cursed by God. Further, the song insinuates the human connection to God, a supreme and supernatural entity.

Next, in *Beowulf*, several narrative shifts bear note, as do Gardner's incorporation of them. The poem begins an explanation of the "fierce spirit's" situation by outlining the Biblical milieu, but in the poem, there is an inexact chronological relationship between the actions of the scop, the historical backdrop, and Grendel's response. Grendel endures hardship "for a time" because "every day" he hears the scop; thus, in the passage which follows this, where the poet describes how the scop recounts the Genesis story, "There he spoke who could relate the beginning of men far back in time, said that the Almighty made earth, a bright field fair in the water that surrounds it, set up in triumph the lights of the sun and the moon . . . " it is unclear whether this occurs on a specific day, many days in a row, or even if Grendel understands the language.

The poet of *Beowulf* then moves forward to the present moment of his tale, the state of affairs at Hrothgar's court prior to Grendel's attacks, "Thus these warriors lived in joy, blessed, until one began to do evil deeds, a hellish enemy. The grim spirit was called Grendel, known as a rover of the borders, one who held the moors, fen and fastness." The placement and use of the pronoun "one" seems significant here, as a listener's immediate

60 (Donaldson, *trans.*, *Beowulf*, 5)

response is to see the "one" as part of the group of happy warriors; this pronominal association between Grendel and the men, insinuating a connection as "one" distinct from "these" yet perhaps in the same group.

As the poet continues his description of Grendel, again not an unsympathetic one, he connects the monster's position to God's judgment of Cain, from the past, "Unhappy creature, he lived for a time in the home of the monster's race, after God had condemned them as kin of Cain. The Eternal Lord avenged the murder in which he slew Abel. Cain had no pleasure in that feud, but He banished him far from mankind, the Ruler, for that misdeed," and so Cain's banishment comes to explain Grendel's roving of the borders.

The next lines imply Grendel's unlucky heritage, "From him [Cain] sprang all bad breeds, trolls and elves and monsters—likewise the giants who for a long time strove with God: He paid them their reward for that," and next the poet goes immediately into the present action of the monster's first attack, "Then, after night came, Grendel went to survey the tall house . . . The creature of evil, grim and fierce, was quickly ready, savage and cruel, and seized from their rest thirty thanes."

In the novel, Gardner uses the poem's narrative situation to highlight his monster's innocence. After hearing the Shaper recount the Genesis story, a passage nearly directly from the poem, Grendel hears the Cain and Abel story for the first time, and Grendel recounts it this way, "He told of an ancient feud between two brothers which split the world between darkness and light. And I, Grendel, was the dark side, he said in effect. The terrible race God cursed. I believed him. Such was the power of the Shaper's harp!" (51) He is still holding the human corpse over his shoulder as this occurs, proof of man's evil toward man.

Just as in the poem, in the novel Grendel has not yet attacked the mead hall when the story of Genesis is told. He may have eaten the occasional human (whether he eats humans prior to his initial attack of the mead hall is unclear in both the novel and the poem) and humans have seen him roving the moors, but he presents neither an immediate nor a pervasive threat. Whereas the Beowulf poet shifts between the chronologies and the explanations, creating an indistinct correlation between the monster's actions and his cursed state,[61] Gardner shows most clearly that Grendel is led to becoming monstrous by the inference of his guilt. During his first encounter with the Shaper in Chapter Three, when he had no history of attacking humans, Grendel's said his heart felt heavy at his "bloodthirsty ways." Similarly, during this encounter, his overactive conscience prompts

---

[61] I believe the *Beowulf* poet does this intentionally.

him to adopt the mantle of Cain's guilt. The Shaper's song tells him that he is quasi-human like the giants, trolls, and "all bad breeds."

Concerning this section of *Beowulf*, Gardner states, "He feels envy and spite . . . perhaps the joy of the Danes would be sufficient alone to infuriate this creature of anguish, but the scop's song, which recalls the time when Grendel's suffering had its beginning, makes things worse."[62] In the poem, the next action is Grendel's first nighttime raid of the mead hall, and it comes after "a time" of endured hardship, presumably when the monster has taken as much as he can take.

By contrast, in Gardner's novel, Grendel's actual first entrance to the group gathered around the Shaper is a quest for mercy, returning their dead to them. While the scene has striking correlations to Beowulf's first battle (his fight with Grendel) and sets up the three-battle parallel between the two works, there are marked differences. Here, in Chapter Four, Gardner establishes Grendel as an actual, not merely ironic or inverted, hero of the novel.

In both cases, the stranger, a foreigner, appears in an effort to quench violence. Beowulf in the poem arrives at Hrothgar's kingdom in order to help the Danes with their problem, the monster which has caused such twelve years of bloodshed. Beowulf and his men trod toward the hall, ("The road was stone-paved, the path showed the way") in order to create harmony, or, as Beowulf tells the coast guard, "In openness of heart I may teach Hrothgar remedy for that, how he, wise and good, shall overpower the foe—if change is ever to come to him, relief from evil's distress—and how his surging cares may be made to cool."[63] Beowulf's strength surpasses any of Hrothgar's court and would be seen as a necessary asset in abetting the monster's cruel attacks.

Likewise, in Chapter Four, Grendel approaches the mead hall prompted by a desire to make the humans recognize the duplicity in singing of peace while destroying one another. His compassion would save the Danes, if only they would hear him, "I staggered out into the open and up toward the hall with my burden, groaning out 'Mercy! Peace!' The harper broke off, the people screamed . . . I sank to my knees crying 'Friend! Friend!'" (51-52). Both Grendel and the corpse he carries (his "burden") become as sacrifices to the human penchant for selfishness, paranoia, and brutality.

Further, Grendel's attempts toward higher ideals are denied him by his appearance as non-human, and the connection between his looks and those who are seen as outcasts. Clearly, the scene illustrates Grendel's endeavor

---

[62] (Gardner, *The Construction of Christian Poetry in Old English*, 67-68)

[63] (Donaldson, *trans., Beowulf*, 8)

to function as a purveyor of "the good," for what else would his calls for mercy, peace, and friendship suggest? Entering the clearing of his adversaries in itself shows arma, while the call for cooperation amidst the humans and urging them toward compassion suggests virum. The body he brings of their dead comrade may be seen as a gift, or at least the recognition of the need to hallow, and not desecrate, the dead: an expression of primus, insofar as it reflects respect for the corporeal, and an instinctive respect for disposition of the dead.[64] At any rate, as a reader one could hardly see his first entrance into their community as malevolent rather than heroic.

Contrast this scene of rejection to Gardner's analysis of the poem, of Beowulf's his arrival at Hrothgar's court. Gardner shows how the human hero reflects all three of the Fulgentian ideals: arma, in his strength, virum in wisdom and loyalty to those even outside his clan, and the understanding of primus as God's sole province.[65]

Grendel in the novel is denied all of this because the humans misapprehend him as strange and monstrous. In fairness to the humans, the situation is complicated by Grendel's lack of self-perception. While he may see himself as a bearer of the idylls of peace, what the humans see (and what readers see as dramatic irony, and yes, dark humor) is a monstrous man-like creature rushing into the gathering carrying a bloody corpse. Thus, his "arma" or valor at rushing into a camp at which he is unknown becomes moot due to his appearance; the virum of advocating peace and compassion is lost, because the message cannot be perceived by men. As for primus, the body he carries over his shoulder, representing the prime material plane, becomes reflective of their worst fears. Rather than enlightening them about their violence, Grendel's entrance provides a focal point for their fears.

In short, they fail to see his truth as opposed to the Shaper's flattering illusions. He receives instead the ironic "reward" for not thinking through the situation and seeing himself accurately: he is attacked. The question here becomes, where lies the fault? In *Beowulf*, the monster's outcast state is explained as a result of God's judgment, but in Gardner's novel does such an explanation suffice? Is a sentient being required to have an understanding of how he may be misperceived, or does the fault lie, at least partially, in the hasty preconceptions of society? If indeed Cowart and Morris are right and the Shaper's virtue leads to an acceptable vision

---

[64] It may also mirror the poem, in Grendel's mother returning for her son's arm.
[65] (Gardner, *The Construction of Christian Poetry in Old English*, 12-1 A)

for mankind to follow, does Grendel's vision of peace and compassion have no place in our world because it isn't presented in a pretty package?

Again, one may see Grendel as an unreliable narrator who revises the story to make himself the hero, yet this would seem to do little more than cast the entire novel and its fake moral center as a joke. Some see it this way, despite compelling evidence to look more deeply. In particular, the correlations between the battles indicate a carefully wrought parallel on Gardner's part. In each case, Beowulf's arrival at Hrothgar's court and Gardner's Grendel entering the enclave, the foreigner's lineage figures largely in the human reaction.

The coast guard in *Beowulf* demands to know the lineage of the Geats; similarly, Hrothgar, on learning Beowulf's name recognizes his family and equates his appearance with the grace of God, "I knew him when he was a boy . . . Holy God of His grace has sent him to us West-Danes, as I hope, against the terror of Grendel."[66] In the novel, the human audience has just heard how Cain's progeny continues to walk the earth as monsters and trolls when Grendel appears among them with a bleeding corpse slung over his shoulder. While in the poem Beowulf is admitted entrance due to Hrothgar's acceptance of his lineage, Grendel in the novel is attacked for the same reasons.

Smaller motifs connect the two works in terms of this first battle, allegorical correlations Gardner has termed linear and vertical in his discussion of the poem. The linear comparisons come by way of the situational similarities. The vertical connections are images and ideas linking the two works. In this case, images of weapons and warfare appear in both scenes. In the poem, spears are equated to Beowulf's heritage, "Spears stood together, seamen's weapons, ash steel-gray at the top. The armed band was worthy of their weapons," and in the novel they become representative of the human's potential harm to Grendel, "I held up the body for protection. Their spears came through it and one of them nicked me . . . I knew by the sting it had venom in it and I understood, as shocked as I'd been the first time, that they could kill me."[67]

The wording of the fighting itself is similar, for in the poem when Beowulf's men attempt to join the fight, it is described thus, " . . . hardy-spirited warriors . . . they thought to hew him on every side"[68] and in the novel "Drunken men rushed me with battle- axes . . . They hacked at me, yipping like dogs."[69] In the poem, Beowulf's ancestry and his choice of

---

[66] (Donaldson, *trans*., *Beowulf*, 9)
[67] (Gardner, *Grendel*, 52)
[68] (Donaldson, *trans*., *Beowulf*, 15)
[69] (Gardner, *Grendel*, 52)

hand-to-hand combat are linked as the fight nears its end, for Grendel's "body would do him no good, for the great-hearted kinsman of Hygelac had him by the hand."[70] Likewise, Gardner's Grendel in this scene acts bear-like, " . . . crushed the body [of the corpse] in my hug, then hurled it in their faces," showing his natural state and connecting him to a bear.[71] The hugging of a bear (to death) will return in Chapter Seven, and connectedness to bears relates, as well, to Beowulf.

The question of identity, functioning on the basic levels in Chapters Two through Four, takes on a more specific quality as the novel continues, as Grendel moves toward adulthood. The child-Grendel's search for acceptance as a member of society becomes the adolescent-Grendel's need to define himself as a dynamic force within his world. The question of Grendel's heritage and the impossibilities of communal love drive him to rashness. Gardner puts it this way: " . . . partly because he is kicked out of the mead hall, he decides to reject the [Shaper's] myth. That's Grendel's hard luck, because when he goes to the mead hall and wants to be a good monster and doesn't want to kill people anymore, Hrothgar's warriors don't know that, and they throw spears at him and hurt him."[72]

In both the poem and the novel, after the fight is over, Grendel runs away. The *Beowulf* poet describes Grendel's flight from the fatal first battle this way, "Grendel must flee from there, mortally sick, seek his joyless home in the fen-slopes."[73] In the novel, Grendel states that he " . . . turned, and fled. They didn't follow. I ran to the center of the forest and fell down panting" (52). To see Grendel as a viable hero in Gardner's novel, not merely an ironic anti-hero, is to see his situation as tragic; the comparison to Beowulf via direct parallel heightens this.

Grendel has no father, to speak of, except in the larger, allegorical sense, and in both the poem and the novel he is equated with the progeny of the doomed. His misery, a direct result of his outcast state, finds no sympathy among his human counterparts. And here lies the catastrophe, one that tortures Grendel through his lifetime but then, through his struggle to achieve identity as part of a sentient community, is turned upon the humans themselves.

Chapters Two through Four show this quite effectively. In Chapter Two, the humans meet Grendel and out of fear they attack him and flee. Chapter Three shows Grendel's continued isolation as he watches

---

[70] (Donaldson, *trans.*, *Beowulf*, 15)

[71] (Gardner, *Grendel*, 52)

[72] Paul F. Ferguson, John R. Maier, Frank McConnell, Sara Matthiessen, "John Gardner: The Art of Fiction LXXIII," in *Conversations with John Gardner*, 150.

[73] (Donaldson, *trans., Beowulf*, 16).

Hrothgar's war-strength grow, and then the Shaper arrives to praise the aggressive plundering, connecting it through his powerful art to notions of a higher power. This in itself would seem to outcast Grendel as surely as did the original poem's scop, casting Grendel as one of the "bad breeds" abhorred by the Almighty. Chapter Four shows the monster trying one more time to claim an identity by entering the encampment and attempting speech. Again, the humans perceive him as monstrous and attack.

The identity which forms for Grendel is thus crafted by the human community itself, through its fear and prejudice, its commercialized art, its perversely warped use of religion to justify violence, and its lack of openness to strangers. Indeed, this would seem a perfect platform from which to launch a diagnosis of modern society's errors.

While Grendel has an abundance of arma, both mightiness of body and bravery, men misperceive it due to his physical appearance: when the shaggy monster enters carrying a bloody corpse, they perceive a threat rather than the moral savior Grendel imagines himself to be. Likewise, Grendel's virum, though including a compassion for fellow beings and a desire to know the truth, does not contain the wisdom of self-reflection needed to understand how the humans will see him and why. What might be called Grendel's moral superiority becomes for the humans, ironically, an image of the darkest terror. And so, at the point in the novel where Grendel reaches maturity, one expects his primus, or place in the world, to be equally miscast.

In some sense, Grendel's primus may be said to be outside human calculations, since he has been raised as a natural creature despite his ability to speak and since he is outside the social order. This defining of a social or material position is as problematic as his capacity to see himself as humans do, since he lacks fellowship and community which might be seen as providing those. Nor may his self-reflection be mitigated by a relationship with God, for he has no formal instruction in religion and the only instruction he may receive, from the humans, seems to categorize him and his kin as outcast from God. The importance of his attempt to affect his circumstances, by entering the community and begging for mercy (Chapter Four), cannot be understated.

The heroism in it, despite its doomed outcome, is not ironic. And while one may fault Grendel for his lack of virum, one may fault as well the humans who have no capacity beyond immediate reaction to their fears: they do not recognize the corpse as a product of their own brutality but shift the blame to Grendel, the perpetrator most obvious because he is unfamiliar to them and therefore foreign. This, then, may be seen as Gardner's critique of one of the failings of modern society. For all intents and purposes, the Shaper's song defines a monster which does not exist and thereby creates one out of a neutral creature whose differences alone alienate him.

Having sensed the presence of something sinister, Grendel leaves the cave and then states, "I went to the cliffwall, then down to the moor . . . I made my mind a blank and fell, sank away like a stone through earth and sea, toward the dragon" (56). Grendel's need to construct a valid identity and establish a place in the world, what may be seen as his reaching for self-knowledge and therefore virum, take him from his attempt to interact with humans toward the dark force of the Dragon. Chapter Five follows an end of Chapter Four which would seem to place the monster in an ambiguous frame of mind if not, actually, in an unreal place.

Grendel, Chapter Five, Surveying the Text

While rams, bulls, twins, and crabs appear in the first four chapters of *Grendel*, corresponding to the astrological sequence of the chapters, a question arises concerning the sign for Chapter Five, Leo the Lion. No lions appear in the chapter, and the only creature is the Dragon, so why does Gardner mean for us to associate the sign with dragons? The lion, king of the forest and a recognizable symbol of superiority, may be applied to the Dragon, which is naturally associated with fire, just as the sign Leo is one of the zodiac's four fire signs. As well, precedent exists for composite mythological creatures sharing qualities of both dragons and lions, for instance in Near Eastern or Mesopotamian cultures.

One such examination has been done by Theodore J. Lewis, who compares the Mesopotamian tale of the god Tishpak to the creature battled in the Ezekiel 32: "These two texts show, in conjunction with other literary sources and iconography, that ancient Near Eastern writers and artists used composite animal imagery—in particular, the juxtaposition of lions and dragons—to demonstrate the preeminence of warriors both human and divine."[74] The reference to Mesopotamian mythology seems obscure until one realizes that Gardner, with translator John Maier edited *Gilgamesh* (published in 1984).[75] Gardner was fully versed in the mythology of Mesopotamia and would've had an excellent resource in Maier, as the two were good friends.

[74] Theodore J. Lewis, "CT 13.33-34 and Ezekiel 32: Lion-Dragon Myths," *Journal of the American Oriental Society,* 116.1 (Jan. - Mar. 1996): 28
[75] John Gardner, *ed.*, and John Maier, *trans.*, *Gilgamesh* (New York: Knopf, 1984)

Gardner's dragon becomes a "composite" symbolically by its structural relation to Leo. As well, in confronting the Dragon despite his terror, Grendel exhibits characteristics of a warrior and so he, too, comes to represent courage. Each time he discredits the Dragon, he is repulsed by insult or condescension, but he keeps at it. When Grendel says, "I think you're lying," the Dragon replies, "I noticed that. You'll never know. It must be very frustrating to be caged like a Chinaman's cricket in a limited mind" (72). As a supernatural being, the Dragon may well read Grendel's mind, be present in his mind, and be present in other places throughout the book, as well as time travel and put spells on others.

Further, Grendel's descriptions of the dragon align him with a supremely powerful serpent and also with a presence that looms and interjects whenever something tragic occurs, which of course implicates the Dragon as a devil figure, reptilian: "Why not?" another mind seems to ask Grendel in the forest, when he thinks of the Shaper as a force for good with mankind (48); "Why not" seems to hiss the darkness, as a phrase, not a question (54); there was a chilly presence, like that of snakes (50); the presence is chilly, combined with images of a snake (50); the presence is "Cold as a dead hand," a "century old presence" and again there is the appearance of a snake (54).

At this point in the novel, the influence of the Shaper's songs on Grendel and the subsequent attack on him by the humans has heightened the ongoing isolation. While Grendel doubts the Dragon's negative apocalyptic vision of the world, the serpent is impressive in all other ways: supremely intelligent, infinitely stronger than Grendel, and an effective rhetorician. More specifically, the Dragon supplies an option to Grendel's identity dilemma, that rather than pay any mind to the Shaper, the world of men, and their God, he should simply continue forward and fully embrace the image of a monster that he appears to be.

As most readers of the novel will agree, the Dragon's advice convinces Grendel to commence his horrific raids on the mead hall. At this point, an important symbolic connection between the elements of the poem and those of the novel exists in the form of a riddle. Gardner comments on the symbolic connections within *Beowulf*: "The poet's main symbol of the doomed world of things physical is the mead hall, where—he insists by verbal repetition—sleep comes after the feast: allegorically, the sleep of death which succeeds the feast of life. This metaphor is urged many times but perhaps also in the name of Hrothgar's hall, "Hart" (also, of course "heart"). While the name fits the horn-curving appearance of the hall, it also recalls for the Christian audience one of Isaiah's chief symbols of the world to be destroyed in the great destruction he foretells, the hart which dragons will devour—a symbol common in medieval Church representations of the end of the world—on columns and panels as well as liturgy and sermon."[76]

Since Gardner supplies his novel with the Dragon who, through his protege Grendel, attempts to destroy the mead hall, an implicit connection to Beowulf the hero exists as well. Evidence of this comes by way of the "hart" (as deer or elk) image superimposed on the arrival of Beowulf in Chapter Nine. Thus the "hart," also the name of Hrothgar's mead hall, becomes the symbolic precursor to Grendel's doom, through the dragon who instructs him to attack it and through Beowulf-as-dragon who will stop Grendel's raids on it. The annihilation of the mead hall by fire, as foretold in the poem, connects as well to the dragon as fire-breather and to the dragon as, in Gardner's novel, the astrological fire sign of Leo the Lion. Such a connection further bolsters the structural correlations between Beowulf's three battles in the poem and Grendel's three battles in the novel.

From the start of the chapter, the Dragon makes clear his superiority and treats Grendel as an apprentice. Grendel, too, describes such a relationship indirectly, "I doubted that I could learn anything from him now" (60). This becomes reiterated by the dragon, who says, "You want the word . . . That's what you've come for" (62). The digression which follows, however, one in which the dragon discusses the relatedness of Time to Space, confuses Grendel. While Grendel argues against the dragon's view of an eventual apocalypse, such a vision being the opposite of a world loved by its Creator (as in the Shaper's songs). At the same time, he cannot find a compromise between the two extremes. He leaves the cave frustrated and feeling foolish, and again having been rejected by a potential role model.

The question for Grendel, then, is how the Dragon's "truth" about an uncaring and godless universe fits with the Shaper's artistic "truth," which he also finds problematic on all levels, "It was a cold-blooded lie that a god had lovingly made the world and set out the sun and moon . . . Yet he, the old Shaper, might make it true, by the sweetness of his harp, his cunning trickery" (55). While Nutter and others strive to posit the Shaper's vision as the novel's (or Gardner's) view of "actual" truth, it seems much more likely that Gardner is investigating Grendel's conflict between two lies which are made to seem true; with no training in art, religion, philosophy, or science, Grendel has only his intuition, and this leads him to recognize the self-serving desires of both of these "mentors."

[76] (Gardner, *The Construction of Christian Poetry in Old English*, 62)

This is not to say that Grendel sees the world as devoid of goodness. Indeed, Grendel sometimes shows a good-natured approach to life in the chapters following the first; his appreciation of ideals such as fairness and compassion are tainted neither by greed nor aspirations to power. In essence, he is as innocent as any creature until he becomes corrupted first by the human value system and then the serpent's.

As well, both the Shaper's songs and the Dragon's philosophies point Grendel in the same direction: to take on the identity of a brutal attacker. His choice, to outcast himself further into the wild and the obscurity of a life void of intellectual or social contact, eschewing both roles and adopting the "peaceable lion" role goes against his character, which is imbued with imagination, curiosity, compassion, and the need to socialize. Ironically, these same attributes, when forced into the only position made available, an enraged reversal, create a monster of terrifying proportions.

John Howell asserts that the Dragon is a psychological projection of Grendel's inner self, "Though Gardner's critics generally discuss the dragon as if he were a character existing apart from Grendel's consciousness, he is in fact Grendel's own dark—or evil—self . . . "[77] Howell sees this as a reflection of Grendel's unconscious, " . . . Grendel looks, as Sartre requires, into his own consciousness and finds 'the dragon,' the incarnation of nihilism . . . Under the influence of this Sartrean Dragon—the 'evil inside' himself—Grendel projects himself as the 'brute existent' by which humanity learns to define itself" (71). For Howell, Grendel becomes a victim of his own inner turmoil, allowing his base inner self to take over. This satisfies questions concerning Grendel's character as well as Gardner's stated desire to show Sartre's philosophies as faulty; as well, it places the novel into a context of modernism or postmodernism.

Even if this is true of Gardner's intentions, it doesn't negate the fact that Gardner expects his readers to see this Dragon as, quite literally, the same beast appearing at the end of *Beowulf.* Grendel's trip to the Dragon must be dream-like because of the great distance between the land of the Geats and the land of the Danes; in the poem, the dragon is in Geatland, and the battle between Beowulf and the dragon takes place decades after Beowulf's trip to the land of the Danes, where Gardner's novel is set. As well, Grendel's journey is dream-like because he has a supernatural connection to the Dragon.

When the Dragon narrates the future for Grendel, he says, "'In a billion billion billion years everything will have come and gone several times, in various forms. Even I will be gone. A certain man will absurdly kill me. A

[77] (John Howell, *Understanding John Gardner*, 69)

terrible pity—loss of a remarkable form of life. Conservationists will howl.' He chuckled" (70). If the Dragon exists only in Grendel's consciousness, it begs the question of how Grendel somehow knows the future (and it also detracts a bit from the joke, or at least gives the novel a more postmodern gloss). Also, the Dragon's philosophical discussion, following the ideas of Alfred Whitehead's philosophies, is so highly scientific and intellectual that Grendel cannot follow it and becomes bored.[78]

Jeff Henderson sees the supernatural aspects of the Dragon as coming from the poem, though he makes a concise list of Gardner's additions to these otherworldly elements. "Grendel's magic invulnerability to weapons—in Gardner's book conferred upon him by the dragon (75)—are such givens of the plot. Among Gardner's additions in this line are the dragon's superhuman intelligence and ability to see all time and space in an instant (62-63) and his telepathic powers whereby he summons Grendel to his cave (56) and reads Grendel's mind during their interview (61). Grendel himself is able to cast a watchdog-silencing spell (136), and he develops precognitive powers of his own which enable him to sense the impending arrival of Beowulf and the Geats (126, 151-152)."[79]

After Grendel leaves the Dragon's cave, he discovers a new immunity to harm from human weapons, though earlier in the book (Chapter Two, Hrothgar's axe and Chapter Four, when he brings in the dead man) humans injure him with their weapons. To see the Dragon as a product of Grendel's mind only (not a supernatural being) is to suppose that Grendel imagines a detailed conversation with a being imminently more intelligent than himself, and then that he leaves this dream state with an inexplicable immunity to weapons.

What might otherwise be Grendel's salvation, an instinctual desire to be part of the group, an inclination toward mercy through connection to other beings and to nature itself, the desire to be understood by others, becomes instead a platform to evil. In fact, Grendel's invulnerability to weapons seems in itself to warp his vicious tendencies, for they no longer threaten or challenge him. The Dragon plays an important part in Grendel's maturation into a monster, for the serpent himself is a representation of materialism and greed: the focal point of his main concerns, his treasure hoard, consists of the jewels and riches of humankind. His advice to Grendel, at the chapter's end, reflects the pointlessness of such an existence,

---

[78] (as Howell also notes, 72)

[79] Henderson, Jeff. "John Gardner's Layered Fiction: The Supernatural and the Paranatural," in *Thor's Hammer: Essays on John Gardner*. (Conway: U of Central Arkansas Press), 167-180

"My advice to you, my violent friend, is to seek out gold and sit on it" (74).

Grendel, Chapter Six, Surveying the Text

Just as Chapter Five is a digression into the philosophies of the Dragon corresponding to one in the poem, Chapter Six consists largely of Grendel's conversation with Unferth, who visits the lair in an attempt to become a hero or else to die a hero, after Grendel has intimidated the Danes in Chapter Four, become emboldened by the Dragon's suggestions, and gone on several nightly raids. This notion of attempting to put into action loyalty to one's leaders, combining heroism, vengeance, and bloodshed, was typical of Anglo-Saxon codes.

Not surprisingly, one finds such themes in the *Beowulf* digression following the Sigemund digression, just as in the novel Unferth's visit to Grendel following Grendel's visit to the Dragon. Similarly, as Leo the Lion captured the spirit of the Dragon, Virgo the Virgin seems an apt characterization of Unferth as the untested hero. As well, the chapter opens with Grendel having survived the rite of passage with the Dragon and moving into the only active role available to him.

In my experience teaching the novel, students invariably confuse this chapter with the next in terms of the astrological connection, for in Chapter Seven Grendel sexually assaults Wealtheow the Queen, whom he has revered for her purity, a motif that readers associate more readily with virginity than with a warrior. Some scholars even point to this as evidence that Gardner's use of the zodiac seems somewhat forced at times. Howell says, "Though the zodiac gave Gardner a structural principle, his philosophical allusions and ideas are only periodically—and then arbitrarily—related to the sun signs" and he adds parenthetically, concerning Chapter Six, "(. . . Gardner actually forces the association by having Grendel pelt apples at Unferth until 'he was crying, only a boy, famous hero or not: a poor miserable virgin.'")[80] When one understands Wealtheow's role in the poem, however, it's clear that she her function in both poem and novel is what Anglo-Saxon's would call a "peace-weaver," as her marriage is meant to bind two tribes. Her children will be central to this, for if she bears children who have blood relation to both tribes, the unity creates strength for all (or at least this is the idea).

However, more specific answers to "Why is *Unferth* the Virgin?" give insights into the workings of the novel. Grendel's depiction of Unferth as

[80] (Howell, *Understanding John Gardner*, 79)

untested sexually and emotionally relates to Grendel's own untested state, both as a being without an appropriate mate and as one in the process of developing an adult identity. The theme of virginity and its undoing begins with the opening lines, which reference Grendel's encounter with the Dragon, "Nothing was changed, everything was changed, by my having seen the dragon. It's one thing to listen, full of scorn and doubt, to poets' versions of time past . . . it's another to know, as coldly as my mother knows her piles of bones, what is" (75). The Dragon provides Grendel's rite of passage, just as Grendel provides the same for Unferth; in both cases, the mentor replaces the neophyte's untested idealism with "the cold truth."

He goes on to describe how the dragon's charm makes him unassailable by weapons. This separation from mankind seems to move him several more steps into the realm of alien being. Later, after the description of his first bloody raids on the mead hall he continues his discussion of his new identity, likening it to a new persona, the creature he perceived his mother to be when she rescued him from the tree (Chapter Two, with images he references), "I was transformed . . . I had become, myself, the mama I'd searched the cliffs for . . . I had become something, as if born again. I had hung between possibilities before . . . now that was passed: I was Grendel, Ruiner of Meadhalls, Wrecker of Kings!" (80). In this loss of innocence and becoming, Grendel matures into the adult form of the creature the humans believe he was born to be (as an offspring of Cain).

Similarly, Unferth arrives at the cave in order to settle the question of Grendel once and for all. In fact, this chapter may be seen as a humorous answer to Beowulf's comment to Unferth in the poem, as he wonders why Hrothgar's mighty warrior didn't vanquish the foe: the answer, supplied here, is that Unferth tried to, but Grendel wouldn't allow it and also wouldn't allow him a hero's death. In Chapter Seven it becomes clear why Gardner established Unferth as "the Virgin" (and saved Wealtheow for the theme of balance).

Describing the prelude to Beowulf's attack on Grendel's mother in the poem, Gardner says, "Throughout the episode, the poet focuses both by literal and by symbolic means on the way in which glory is kept or lost" and Unferth, he states, reflects the failure of a code reflected brilliantly in his better, Beowulf." As an example, Gardner emphasizes the importance of the exchange between Unferth and Beowulf at the edge of the mere, with Hrunting serving as a symbol, "The symbolic contrast to Beowulf is the sword Hrunting. Whereas Beowulf proves true, the sword proves inadequate . . . Like Unferth, the sword 'his dom alaeg.'" Like Unferth, the sword has well-known virtues but is not up for the task set for it this time." Beowulf in the poem fulfills this code, and, as Gardner points out, he foils Unferth through his innate heroism, " . . . In the fight which Beowulf does have the valor and wisdom to undertake, the poet continually emphasizes the way Beowulf keeps his wits, his valor, and his awareness of the value of true fame, the lawful man's form of glory."[81]

Along those lines, we see in this chapter the full effect of the Dragon on Grendel, for he has become distinctly cruel, not simply misunderstood or enraged. His measured and evil treatment of Unferth, keeping him alive for sport, with Unferth's attempts to disguise himself and be killed anyway, show that Grendel has taken to heart the Dragon when he says, "You improve them, my boy!" (72) By refusing Unferth any outlet for his aggression or adoption of the hero's role, Grendel ruins him the only way he could be ruined, just as the Shaper (through his rendition of the Old Testament regarding Cain) does the same to Grendel.

Gardner's description of the first mead hall visit and the second correspond to images from the poem, with Grendel going to hear the Shaper's song and feeling anger at the overconfidence of humans and their so-called connection to God. While listening this time, after having met with the dragon, but before his raids have begun (76) he is once more attacked by a guard. Grendel prefaces the beginning his raids with this explanation, "I'd meant them no harm, but they'd attacked me again, as always. They were crazy" (79). The dragon's charm and the new disconnect from mankind sends him further into wrath; as well, their frightful response to the gore widens this gulf and spurs him to greater heights of horror. While he describes the manic glee of the bloody decapitations, he points out as well his solitary anguish: "But also, as never before, I was alone" (80).

Similarly, in *Beowulf*, Unferth may be one of Hrothgar's thanes, but he is atypical and distinctly alone. It is reported that he killed his brothers out of jealousy, which likens him to Cain (a connection to Grendel). Gardner, discussing Beowulf's first entry into Heorot in the poem, with its profusive imagery of cups overflowing with mead, references Unferth in passing, saying that some might interpret the cups as Eucharistic, however, " . . . these cups are *not* Eucharistic: they make men 'beore druncne,' so that a man like Beowulf who never gets drunk and slays kinsmen is worthy of remark."[82] Unferth, by contrast, remains unworthy. His jealous attempt to malign Beowulf's reputation, calling into question the hero's

---

[81] (Gardner, *The Construction of Christian Poetry in Old English*, 77-79)
[82] (Gardner, *The Construction of Christian Poetry in Old English*, 84)

recount of slaying sea monsters with Brecca, seems typical. In response, as Beowulf points out, if Unferth had done his job well, he'd have vanquished Grendel or died at the monster's hands; as a warrior, then, Unferth remains untested and alive, compared to the multitude of thanes whom Grendel killed in the twelve years of his raids.

Further, both Unferth and Grendel make attempts at adopting the role handed them by the human community. Like Cain, neither Unferth nor Grendel can assimilate fully into society, to some extent due to a stigma but largely as a result of their jealousy and anger. For Gardner, the use of Unferth as an ironic foil to his monster-hero allows certain questions from the poem a new perspective—and this, in the context of virginity, creates for both Grendel and Unferth an "un-cast" as well as "outcast" persona. Grendel isn't allowed into Hrothgar's court (or his mead hall) except as its destroyer. Unferth, on the other hand, is one of Hrothgar's warriors, but because he does not have Beowulf's unnatural strength, never mind the grace of God, he could not possibly eradicate Grendel.

In the novel, Grendel's having become the destroyer has nearly ruined him, "But though I laughed, I felt trapped, as hollow as a rotten tree . . . I saw myself swelling like bellows on their blood, a meaningless smudge in a universe dead as old wind over bones, abandoned except for the burnt-blood scent of the dragon" (81-82). Unferth now enters and becomes what Grendel refers to as, " . . . a crowning absurdity, my salvation that moment" (82). Grendel has lost his innocence and become an uncontrolled terror, so what makes Unferth a savior? The explanation comes in the unfolding scene, in Unferth's realization that he and Grendel speak the same language.

The connection of the human heroism to Grendel-as-hero comes subtly in the description, "I saw my mother moving slowly and silently past me, blue murder in her eyes . . . My mother moved back and forth like a bear behind me . . . " (86). The folktale link between "bear's son" and Beowulf now directly applies to Grendel as the "bear's son." Even as Unferth expounds on notions of heroism, Grendel listens unmoved. Nor, clearly, are the readers meant to see this scene as given through a warped perspective: Unferth elicits humor, not respect, as ineffectual here as in the poem—perhaps more so, since here he may communicate with Grendel.

The power of speech, like the Shaper's art, becomes little more than an exercise in hypocrisy, coupled with the pretense of high ideals. The entire time Unferth lectures Grendel could be used to bargain with him, or question him, or at the very least to beg his mercy on the mead hall. Even when Grendel gives him the benefit of the doubt, "I thought he would laugh at the bottomless stupidity of my cynicism" (89), Unferth instead makes a pathetic argument in favor of meaningless heroic acts. Next, he threatens to commit suicide if Grendel refuses to kill him, and then he falls asleep. The heroism of which he boasts (as flimsy as the Shaper's ideals), are typified in the chapter's most humorous moment, when after he falls asleep Grendel carries him back to the mead hall unharmed (though he kills a sleeping guard to make his point).

Even so, the power of the speech act comes to a new height in the novel here. As Grendel's desire to manifest his ego in the world grows, the only one with whom he's able to communicate with is the Dragon. The theme of Grendel's becoming may be seen as related to the changing role of language as the novel progresses, as seen in the following analysis. Gardner starts with Grendel in his last days, a creature who, in frustration and loneliness, shouts orders at natural creatures who cannot understand him, and who then goes on to rail at the uncomprehending trees and sky. As the novel flashes back to Grendel's childhood, one sees how this attempt to communicate becomes paradigmatic with the evolution of his isolation. Chapters Two, Three, and Four highlight the danger in Grendel's situation, a character unable to make himself understood to those who perceive him as a threat.

In Chapter Two, Hrothgar and the gathered humans mistake his hunger cry as a threat, and then in Chapter Four he attempts to reconcile dichotomies between the beauty of the Shaper's poetry and the violence of men, but is misunderstood as he enters their camp crying "Mercy! Peace!" (51) and then "Friend! Friend!" (52). In both cases, the humans attack him. As for the Shaper's poetry, Chapter Three shows Grendel being moved by the power of words, "ridiculous hairy creature being torn apart by poetry," (44) with no means of communicating his angst, resulting in his shrieking in pain and running homeward "on all fours" (45). This return to his natural habitat does not assuage his pain: rather, his mother's inability to speak or understand language is a continual source of frustration for Grendel, suggesting his isolation from her as well and hindering his capacity to identify with her. In an ironic twist on existentialism, he can't even explain to her that he doesn't believe she exists.

With Chapters Five and Six, however, a major transformation occurs, for both the Dragon and Unferth understand Grendel's diction well enough to hold sophisticated conversations with him. Grendel's interaction with the Dragon in Chapter Five may be seen as an example of how the search for identity may lead to corruption, just as his discussion in Chapter Six shows how Unferth's adoption of a heroic stance or creed does not necessarily lead to valor or even enlightenment. As Grendel's desire to manifest his ego in the world grows, the only one with whom he's able to communicate with is the Dragon. The theme of Grendel's becoming may be seen as related to the changing role of language as the novel progresses. While the Dragon's philosophy nearly undoes Grendel, Unferth's ridiculous speeches and his ability to speak with Grendel, becomes an absurd salvation, lifting Grendel from horrific isolation to something like absurd salvation.

In Chapter Six, Unferth's behavior in going to Grendel's cave reflects heroic virtues until he lapses into self-pity after discussing suicide and then falls asleep. On seeing Grendel again at the mead hall on the monster's subsequent attacks, Unferth's behavior slides even further from heroic grace: his attempts at a glorious "death by Grendel" include dressing as an old woman and a dog, clearly nothing like Beowulf's apprehension of "the value of true fame" in the poem.[83] This activity in Chapter Six, therefore, allows Gardner to set up the situation for the second battle, not between the hero and Grendel's mother, but between the antihero and the mother of future Danish kings. In setting up the situation, he mirrors, inverts, and reinvents the particulars of the poem.

As well, in the poem, Unferth's failure to protect his people, his untested and virgin heroism, becomes a foil to Beowulf's heroic code—indeed, it creates the need for the intervention of a foreign hero. In the case of the second battle, the testing of Beowulf's masculinity against a female opponent creates the sexual metaphor of the sword as penis, as Chance's analysis seeks to show. Hrunting proves "impotent against the charm or spell of the 'sword-greedy' woman" and so Beowulf selects one of the Giant's swords, "an appropriate tool to quell such a woman" (259). Similarly, in Chapter Six of the novel, Unferth as virgin reflects the impotence of the heroic code. In Chapter Seven, this powerlessness is magnified. When Grendel attacks Wealtheow, "No one would defend her, not even suicidal Unferth at the door, screaming his rage—self-hatred" (108).

In both works, once the female enters the situation and causes an imbalance, internally for the protagonist, externally via the liaisons she represents, this heroic virginity is called to the test. Grendel decides then not to kill "hero" Unferth, ever, but instead pelts him with apples (fairly obvious symbol of lost innocence), shaming him instead. The serpent-dragon tempts Grendel to become a new destroyer and Unferth's naive heroism becomes an obvious victim. He "saves" Grendel from the boredom of isolation and yet, in negating Unferth's heroism here and later in the chapter, Grendel enlarges his capacity for monstrous behavior from

---

[83] (Gardner, *The Construction of Christian Poetry in Old English*, 77)

the purely physical to the intellectual. The chapter ends with Grendel having emerged into his own maturity, adopted by the serpent dragon and humans alike as the new and undeniable brute existent to disrupt Hrothgar's world.

Dragons in Digression

Beowulf scholars have long debated the importance of the digressions away from the central action of the poem. Questions arise among scholars concerning the work's structure, especially since the digressions suspend the narrative action of what might be called the poem's "present moments" (Beowulf's battles with Grendel, Grendel's mother, and the dragon). While early scholars suggest the poem's conglomerate qualities as evidence of its disunity, seeing the poem as written by multiple authors over a period of time, this idea has largely been replaced with the belief that the epic was crafted by a single poet with a single vision. This begs the question of how the lengthy digressions fit within the plot.

Adrien Bonjour provides intriguing possibilities, suggesting a poetic purpose to the many interludes between the narrative actions of the poem. Bonjour agrees with Tolkien's claims concerning the poem's inherent literary value, and argues against those who would see the poem's digressions as evidence of an inferior art. He posits the idea of such interludes as, themselves, necessary to the narrative's progression. Bonjour cites Klaeber on the poem's separate points of construction, Klaeber seeing the opening of the poem with its glorification of Scyld as part of the Grendel encounter but completely discreet from the dragon episode. While Klaeber would see this as evidence of the poem's disunity, Bonjour applauds its thematic purposes. To begin with the notion of a great peoples ruled by a great king is to discount any perceived weaknesses on the part of Hrothgar and the Danes, thereby making Beowulf's achievement all the greater.

Bonjour sees the discussion of Scyld's ascension to power as both a parallel to Beowulf's gathering greatness and, more importantly, perhaps, a foreshadowing of Beowulf's ultimate demise: communities need great heroes to lead them out of danger, to battle horrific monsters, and when they don't have them, chaos ensues. Beowulf, like Scyld, comes out of nowhere and saves the Danes; like Scyld, his might becomes known and he becomes a great king; like Hrothgar, he is faced with horrors that threaten his people; like the Danes, the Geats need a hero who can help their aging king overcome his foe. That the Geats do not have one, and that Beowulf's death comes even as he kills the dragon, is part of the poem's message—not as tidy as a happy ending, to be sure, but certainly not distinct from the poem's thematic context, as Bonjour sees it.

Bonjour treats the poem's other digressions as well. He uses a thought-provoking questioning of the poet's choices, such as which type of information the poet includes about Beowulf's father and why: Hrothgar does not merely praise Beowulf's background and heritage, but instead mentions a situation in which Beowulf's father was helped by the Danes. In doing so, the notion of reciprocity is reinforced, along with underlying reasons for Beowulf's decision to come to Denmark. Digressions in the poem illuminate the present situation of conflict Beowulf will face. Thus, for Bonjour as well as for Gardner, the interludes and digressions function as relevant indicators of the cultural value codes within the actual heroic contests.[84]

Principally, such digressions highlight important elements of conflict relating to personal character and choice—or, as Gardner refers to them in the poem, arma, virum, and primus. This notion becomes important when one turns to Gardner's novel and its digressions. Both Chapter Five and Six may be seen as extended digressions concerning the nature of one's place in the world, or how arma and virum function to establish one's primus. As Grendel grows from childhood, in Chapters One through Four, Gardner shows how the monster's attributes, though positive or certainly neutral in and of themselves, are misperceived by humans and therefore cast in a negative light.

Gardner himself opposed any notion of the poem lacking structural integrity: "We have no grounds for an *a priori* assumption that Beowulf is, as even Tolkien thought, a poem which has inconsistencies, not a 'tight' work of art. Its disjunctive and digressive nature is by no means proof of confusion or corruption by interpolation, as nearly all recent critics agree. The digressions make sense." He goes on to recount the literary history as basis for such digressions, and labels them, "Moreover, both in pre-Christian and in Christian poetry from Anglo-Saxon times we have instances of what might be called poetic mosaic, or, as some recent critics say, "interlace"[85]: that is to say we find poems made up largely of old materials woven together for a new aesthetic purpose." Finally, he says that while this style can be found in a historical survey of Christian poetry, "We do have grounds, on the other hand, for a hypothesis that the poem is

---

[84] Adrien Bonjour *Digressions in Beowulf* (Oxford: Basil Blackwell, 1965), a work Gardner references in *The Construction of Christian Poetry in Old English*).

[85] Gardner refers to John Leyerle's "The Interlace Structure of *Beowulf*," a well-known article and one Gardner cites in *The Construction of Christian Poetry in Old English*.

the systematic allegorization of pagan material, as such critics as McNamee and Nicholson maintain. If this hypothesis is right, we ought to be able to find the system complete, uncontradicted, and emphatic—that is, obvious once we have the key."[86]

Chapter Five of the novel is a digression. It relates to the monster's identity as he tests notions of moral and social responsibility, community, and heroism, against the Dragon's unrelenting negativity, even as he searches for his role in the cosmos. It halts the present action of the novel following Grendel's first violent combat with humans. If Gardner sees *Beowulf's* digressions as "old materials woven together for a new aesthetic purpose," and Bonjour is correct that such interludes highlight the conflict faced by the hero, it makes perfect sense in Chapter Five for Gardner to include a digression on the Dragon's (evil) code of existence.

Indeed, the entire chapter is a complex, extended monologue on atheism and the futility of morals, an endorsement of materialistic carpe diem in which a creature as powerful as the Dragon finds its greatest contentment in hoarding a pile of treasure. This perspective also corresponds to the actions and belief system of Hrothgar and the Danes, at least as Grendel chronicles their behavior.

Further, as confirmation that Gardner means to have created a parallel between the three battles in both works, it bears more than passing mention that in the poem, the digression immediately following Beowulf's first battle is in fact the story of Sigemund, the famous dragon slayer. This foreshadows Beowulf's eventual third battle, his fatal encounter with the dragon, just as Chapter Five of *Grendel* foreshadows Grendel's third and fatal battle, the Beowulf (with wings who spouts fire) who teaches him "the wall is hard," as proof that Sartre's existentialism is not enough to keep one alive.

Unferth as the Moral Hero in *Grendel*? Unlikely.

As I discussed in the section "Gardner Scholars, the Shaper, and *On Moral Fiction*," a number of scholars place *Grendel* with Gardner's other novels, and then locate it within his statements about the morality of art by arguing that some other character in the novel (not the monster) is the hero. Along with the Shaper, Unferth has been allotted this role. It may be helpful to revisit Unferth's role in the poem, and then Gardner's discussion of him, role before moving to the novel and his essays.

---

[86] (Gardner, *The Construction of Christian Poetry in Old English*, 60-62)

Upon Beowulf's introduction at Hrothgar's court in the poem, Unferth feels challenged by the great hero because none of the Danes have been able to conquer Grendel. In berating tales of a sea monster killing contest between Beowulf and Brecca, Unferth means to foretell the Geat's downfall by Grendel. About this digression, Bonjour states that Unferth can neither accept Grendel as a monster that could be defeated by a mortal, nor accept Beowulf as a hero with nearly supernatural powers. The presentation of the Brecca story reveals not merely Unferth's abject jealousy but also Beowulf's superiority for, as Bonjour states, " . . . by contrast, the effect of Beowulf's counter-attack gains in force. It reduces to naught the traces of misgivings and at the same time effectively illustrates and emphasizes Beowulf's capacities, already implied in the first episode"[87] (22).

Similarly, Gardner describes the situation of Unferth's digression as one with import to the poem's current action, "Now Unferth . . . trouble-making priest of Woden . . . enters the poem primarily to foil Beowulf's virum: Unferth is mistaken in his facts," and goes on to say that Unferth is provoked, " . . . by wrath and (to the Christian audience) erroneous religion, and is drunk. In other words, his reasoning is ill-grounded, and his irascible and concupiscent souls are faulty."[88]

As for the novel, Nutter reflects on the heroism of Unferth in Chapter Six and beyond, calling the thane's actions the manifestation of the Shaper's visions; that Unferth follows Grendel back to his cave and does not give up his quest to kill the monster suggests a value system worth emulating. Nutter goes on to say that while Gardner would see Unferth's position as "too sentimental and too romantic," "he . . . would also affirm the basic intuition of Unferth's statements about heroism and the artistic vision that led him to want to emulate the heroic ideal: namely, as he argues in *On Moral Fiction*, that art 'designs visions worth trying to make fact.'" As well, he says, "What Gardner attempts to do in his fiction is provide models to be emulated, but in such a way that life's tragedies are also enumerated in the overall accounting of human life."[89]

Though it attempts to reconcile the darkness of Grendel's actions with the principles in Gardner's theories, this reading nonetheless results in aligning Gardner's views with Unferth, a character who—in the poem—stands as ethical counterpoint to the great Beowulf, not only as the murderer of his own kin, but also as a jealous and vindictive drunkard who redeems himself only after Beowulf kills Grendel (by giving the ancestral

[87] (Bonjour, *Digressions in Beowulf*, 22)
[88] (Gardner, *The Construction of Christian Poetry in Old English*, 73)
[89] (Nutter, *A Dream of Peace*, 70-72, 100)

sword Hrunting to Beowulf for the battle with Grendel's mother.) Gardner himself refers to Unferth indirectly in contrasting him to Beowulf's distinctions as a hero, " . . . a man like Beowulf who never gets drunk and slays kinsmen is worthy of remark."[90]

In addition, it posits some unlikely assumptions about Gardner's view of the poem. One cannot imagine he would be pleased to have his tenets in *On Moral Fiction* compared to Unferth's heroic virtues, as seen in either the poem or the novel. Nor is Nutter the only Gardner scholar whose application of moral order to the novel would seem to add positive attributes onto human beings whom Grendel so aptly critiques. Leonard Butts sees Grendel as a failed artist, with Chapter Six, which suggests his views on the world to be naive and untested.[91]

In fact, Butts would seem to claim Unferth as a hero, not merely a martyr: "Just as the moral artist creates on one level to assuage feelings of guilt and fear, Unferth seeks a hero's death because he is literally a Cain-figure, having killed his brother. Grendel's refusal to allow him a redeeming and heroic death only increases Unferth's feelings of guilt and shame, but what Unferth does not understand is that by continuing to live in the shadow of the darker vision represented by Grendel, he becomes more of a hero, for, despite his suffering, Unferth endures" (93-94).

Like Nutter and Butts, Morris allies Unferth with Gardner's ideals on virtue as seen elsewhere "Grendel abandons value and morality and pitches toward nihilism, laughing all the while at Unferth's (and Gardner's) notions of man's potential for brilliance . . . Though Unferth exaggerates a bit (there is certainly meaning to the world beyond the hero), he is basically true to Gardner's belief in the significance of the hero (a belief demonstrated, for example, in *The Wreckage of Agathon* and *Freddy's Book*)."[92] While it is true that Grendel scoffs at Unferth's ideas about heroism, he does so in the context of Unferth's failure as a man. The concept of heroism that he espouses seems to be based less on honor or love of God or even commitment to the community than it does on his lack of anything else in his life. In his isolation, jealousy, and self-loathing, he is closer morally to Grendel than to anyone else in the novel, except that Grendel at least (in his discussion with the Dragon) sought some way to avoid the life path he was being shuttled toward, while Unferth seems to be embracing his at all costs.

---

[90] (Gardner, *The Construction of Christian Poetry in Old English*, 84)

[91] Leonard Butts, *The Novels of John Gardner* (Baton Rouge: Louisiana State UP), 93-94

[92] (Morris, *A World of Order and Light,* 62)

Unferth is not without aspects of bravery, just as Grendel's courage showed in the Dragon's space. Chapter Six might be seen as both a parallel and an inversion of Chapter Five, with Grendel being visited by Unferth, who explains concepts of heroism—Unferth trying to prove himself heroic—and Grendel scoffing at the idealism. In both chapters the visitor braves great risks to face a threatening creature of a separate species in its own habitat; the creature maintains an aloof distance, unpersuaded by arguments for social order and so-called moral action. Similarities of a more subtle nature are present as well: while Grendel blanks his mind to go to the dragon, Unferth falls asleep after having seen Grendel. Further, the central thematic thread in these two chapters rests on notions of personal identity and communal function.

Several factors operate here. The functions may be defined by what might be termed an occupational standard—specifically, how value systems combined with action determine whether one is a "monster" or a "hero." As well, both chapters contain the notion of a deeper sense of identity through circumstance and nature. In Anglo Saxon terms, this may be defined as emanating from fate or doom, while in modern times we tend to quantify an individual's situation as a function of their environment. In the poem, the fact of Grendel lacking a father removes him from the patriarchal system so important to the society of Hrothgar and Beowulf. As a result, the explanations of his lineage connect him to Cain and the doomed descendants of Cain.

In *Beowulf* (and in the novel), the poet points out Biblical divisions which alienate creatures like Grendel. Despite this difference of perspective, there are points of connection, fascinating in themselves—such as the poet's empathy for Grendel (and Grendel's mother) which acknowledges their humanness, or how Gardner's protagonist questions whether the cosmos is random or systematic, which contains notions of fate, doom, and the existence (or non- existence) of a controlling force (or God). Similarly, the poem shows Unferth as a man whose past crimes alienate him from other men, but who is able to admit his mistakes and then offer his family's ancestral sword to Beowulf prior to the battle with Grendel's mother.

In Chapters Five and Six, Grendel's identity as unfulfilled due to his outcast state parallels the Dragon, as both are monsters apart from and feared by the world of men, but it parallels Unferth as equally, an unfulfilled hero separated from his peers due to having murdered his brothers. The inquiry of identity surveyed as a matter of self-awareness in the earlier chapters of Gardner's novel becomes a question of one's place in the world as defined by relationship to community and, within this, one's vocation as either protector or destroyer. On another level, the Shaper's songs which spell out the division of good and evil in the universe, and God's role as master of the good, would seem to demand such a dichotomy. Certainly, the Dragon as tempter and devil fits this, just as Unferth's murder of his brothers equates him to Cain, and both then may be seen as connected to Grendel as exiled by God.

Further, Grendel's trepidation over the Shaper's art and its apparent hypocrisies leads him to the Dragon's lair in the first place and becomes one of the principal topics of their conversation. One may argue that the Shaper's art inspires Unferth as well, as Nutter says,[93] for the thane's notions of heroism seem to parallel the Shaper's songs as Grendel references them. Still, to see Unferth as a paradigm of virtue connected to Gardner's view of "man's potential for brilliance" (Morris) seems to be stretching the point more than a little.

Most Gardner scholars focus on what they see as the moral polarities of the novel rather than on Grendel's evolution as a character, so they see the Shaper and Dragon as polar opposites. Butts states, "Since Grendel lacks imagination, he cannot distinguish between the manipulation of language for good (the Shaper's poetry) and the manipulation of language for evil (the dragon's philosophical argument)."[94] This begs the question of how Grendel may be perceived as lacking in imagination, but it seems also to evade the issue of the Shaper's dishonesty: is it his manipulation of language or his manipulation of humans *through* language that creates the apparent "good"? Indeed, the Shaper's manipulation of language inspires an entire people toward their more warlike instincts, the opposite of Grendel's call for mercy and peace.

Similar to Butts, Nutter sees the Shaper's vision as one which "saves" Hrothgar's people,[95] and he notes how the Dragon disparages the vision as a lie. Problematically for Nutter, perhaps, his depiction of the Dragon's disparaging the Shaper as seen here, "The reality the Shaper places before them is just an illusion, the dragon insists, but a successful one in that it manages to keep the people going from generation to generation" (68) sounds amazingly similar to Gardner's own account of the Shaper's role, "The Shaper comes along in a meaningless, stupid kingdom and makes up a rationale. He creates the heroism, the feeling of tribal unity. He makes the people brave. And sure, it's a lie, but it's also a vision."[96] In a later interview, Gardner states this unequivocally: " . . . the shaper, the scop, the court poet comes to this horrible court that's made itself what it is by

---

[93] (Nutter, *A Dream of Peace*, 70)

[94] (Butts, *The Novels of John Gardner*, 91)

[95] (Nutter, *A Dream of Peace*, 68)

[96] (Bellamy interview, *Conversations with John Gardner*, 15)

killing everybody, beating people, chopping them to death, and the poet looks at this havoc around him and makes up a story about what a wonderful court it is, what noble ideals it has. The courtiers are just dumb enough to believe it . . . "[97] Note how Gardner's view allies with Grendel's on this.

Insofar as the Dragon convinces Grendel that the humans need monsters to challenge them and make them better, the Shaper's songs also involve humans taking up arms and conquering their foes; when Grendel steps into the role of their greatest foe, he is answering these similar mantras and not, as some would have it, choosing between good and evil. This is the problem with viewing the novel as a polarity of morals, and then equating it with Gardner's ideas about morality and art: it naturally leads one to posit the Shaper's view as properly moral, or to see Unferth as the human epitome of heroism in the book.

Structurally, the approach leads to a somewhat simplistic perception of the novel, both morally, with the "good Shaper" exemplifying the devoutly religious author of the *Beowulf* poem and the "bad dragon" representing the voice of nihilism from the Modern Age, and with this a fallacy of construction, with Grendel necessarily a victim only, excluded from the "good" Shaper and tricked by the "bad" Dragon. In such an approach, the novel seems to be a philosophical treatise meant to support a god-centered view of the universe as posited by the Shaper opposed by the self-centered view as posited by the dragon, with Grendel moving from goodness to evil as a result of his naive misperceptions.

Next, it proves useful to investigate the connections between the allegory in the poem, as Gardner saw it, and the allegory he presents in the ironic reinvention of the poem's first monster as protagonist. In Gardner's view, the *Beowulf* poet focuses on how living correctly leads to gain, with God or "Wuldor-cyning" as ruler analogous to a Germanic chieftain, just as in Caedmonic verse. In *Beowulf*, the Fulgentian virtues, alone or in combination, allow the abiding of laws to equate with respect and abundance on all levels. The poem diverges from its predecessors in what Gardner describes thus: "The difference, central to the poem's meaning, is that the earthly king works within the intransigent limits of mutability: all things physical are doomed." The mead hall represents, Gardner says, this doomed world.[98] By writing *Grendel* from the perspective of doom's enactor—one who, like Grendel in the poem, has no active relationship with God (indeed, Gardner's Grendel disdains the notion)—Gardner

[97] (Ferguson interview, *Conversations with John Gardner*, 150)

[98] (Gardner *The Construction of Christian Poetry in Old English* 61-62)

provides a secular view on the notion of human calamity. The humans suffer because of their paranoid selfishness. Grendel suffers because he cannot rise above their paranoid perceptions, eventually adopting their view of him as his own.

In Gardner's novel, strictly speaking, formal notions of God as Creator complicate the matter, for through the Shaper they infuse the Danes with notions of their own invulnerability, and they heighten the paranoia against outsiders. For Grendel as well such a paradigm exists. In merely adopting these ideas as his own, he fails to see a true morality and begins to consider himself evil, and then to become evil. The Dragon helps him along in this process, but the Dragon is not the core of the problem. The irony here has to do with society and community, and the equation of such societal codes to ethical codes of conduct. The Shaper gives the Danes two apparent choices, to accept themselves as created by God and thereby within His auspices and protection, or to see themselves as part of the outcast kin of Cain, a dangerous position, for it encompasses all of those outside of their chieftain Hrothgar's domain.

It's important to note the differences between the way the humans see themselves prior to the Shaper's arrival in Chapter Three and their perspectives as altered by his poetry. While Grendel's description of them in the earlier chapters shows them wedded to greed and violence as a means of gain, the Shaper's art does more than simply validate this lifestyle. Indeed, the narrative of Cain and Abel, in both the poem and the novel, follows Creation as an example of God's condemnation of murder (and the greed or jealousy which results in murder). God casts out Cain because he violates the religious ethic. Rather than seeing this as an invective against greed, jealousy, and murder (with an exhortation to follow the code and treat one another with respect), the Shaper's art convinces them to take the meaning literally—to see themselves as beloved by God while doubling down against any outcasts, outsiders who, like Cain, are not merely of a different tribe, but who are "outside" because of their sins.

The idea of reward through correct living becomes a reflective judgment on any who seem to be lacking such rewards. The human society, to which Grendel so desperately aspires, shuns all outsiders (as did many in the Anglo-Saxon world), a stance that is increased by the Shaper's art, not decreased. In seeking his true adult identity, Grendel comes face to face with the Dragon and Unferth, both of whom are symbols of moral failure. The Dragon, with his unmitigated materialism and scorn of goodness, clearly has allegorical associations with the devil; like Satan, he inspires Grendel to seek power. Unferth, who has murdered his own kin, represents Cain on the basic level, but also in a more complex way. Grendel's refusal to let Unferth sacrifice his life parallels the refused sacrifice of Cain.

Grendel who himself has been rejected by the humans on several occasions, uses rejection as a means of power over Unferth. In this way, he becomes connected to both the Dragon and to Unferth, and, as well, connects them to one another. He may be seen, at this point in the novel, as a kind of "double Adam," for he has been tempted by the Dragon into disregarding notions of a moral universe (temptations to which he has succumbed at least partially because the Shaper's visions are composed of lies); in adopting his new identity, Grendel accepts the Shaper's title of "Cain's kin." At the end of Chapter Six, he refuses Unferth, representative of Cain, the only sacrifice allowed by his society: a heroic death. An examination of these two chapters reveals how the allegory of Beowulf becomes reinvented within a world where God's voice or any other voice calling for "Mercy!" and "Peace!" cannot be heard. Grendel's need for identity moves him toward a society which rejects him, unless he becomes a monster, and moves him away from his own more peaceable nature.

This posit in itself is life affirming and conforms to Gardner's ideas about moral art, for it shows the difficulties faced by outcasts. Modern life, if one sees the novel as representative, is more complex than a division of good and evil. One must be vigilant against art that panders (the Shaper), seeming experts who encourage nihilism (the Dragon), and false heroes (Unferth).

CHAPTER THREE

BATTLE TWO: ETERNAL MATERNAL FEMININE

Maternity's Role in the Second Battle, Divided into Episodes One and Two Defined

Chapter Seven of *Grendel* contains two distinct episodes involving Wealtheow, just as the poem contains two distinct episodes concerning Grendel's mother. Beowulf in the poem and Gardner's Grendel are alike in their symbolic role as combatants of these females. In each work, the first section devoted to the female (which I'll call Episode One), attempts to define her role as child-bearer, one for whom the blood connection to the child creates specific loyalties of kinship. In the poem, after Grendel's death, his mother enters the mead hall on a mission to retrieve the arm of her dead son that has been hung over the mantle as a trophy. She kills Aescher in the process, but her intentions are clearly tied to fealty with her child. In the novel, Wealtheow is given in trade to Hrothgar in order to avert war, with the idea that the marriage will produce children and unite the two tribes in peace.

The second section concerning the female (Episode Two), shows the male lead character of each work as an enemy tribe's combatant to the female. He challenges the female's role and overcomes her in an act of force wherein her sexuality becomes central. More specifically, he enters her lair and flaunts the weakness of her kinship by dominating her. In this way, while her child-bearing role at the height of her prime (primus) would have highlighted her blood loyalty (virum), the male uses his might (arma) to assault her and dishonor such a link. In specific terms, the poem's Episode Two has Beowulf step in to save the humans by going to the lair of Grendel's mother and killing her with a sword of the Giants, while in the novel Grendel disrupts the established peace by entering the mead hall and sexually assaulting Wealtheow in front of her kin. In each case, the title character dominates his enemies by negating the honor of the female's role.

Prior to the attack, as the poem and the novel each enter the first phase of this battle, Episode One, the protagonists are confronted with a female whose roles contain polarities. The conflict between opposing sides underscores the contradictions inherent in each of the females. The roles of "mother," "lover," "wife," and especially "other" can each be applied to both Grendel's mother (in the poem) and Wealtheow (in the novel). While Grendel's mother in the poem is often referred to as "the second monster," Jane Chance, among others, points to the *Beowulf* poet's use of various linguistic terms in his descriptions of Grendel's mother, such as a "Queen," "a lady," and "a woman of high rank." In Chance's view, this sets up the parody or the "inversion" of the "ideal Anglo Saxon woman."[99]

Gardner observed, albeit referencing the third movement, " . . . the significance of queens becomes explicit. They are the peace weavers—love is raised to national strategy," although he adds, mentioning Beowulf's discussion and Hildeburh's tale, "not even love—that is, not human love—is sufficient to turn away disaster."[100] In *Grendel*, Gardner uses the maternal peace-weaver as the foil of intentions (Hrothgar's, in the first episode, as the army arrives to annihilate Hygmod's tribe, and Grendel's in the second episode, with his attack on Wealtheow following the joyous celebration of unity between the factions), as he has used Unferth as a symbol of thwarted heroism. While Grendel is attracted to Wealtheow, he also sees her as the Queen and mate of his enemy. Leonard Butts notes that Grendel sees a resemblance between his mother's type of unthinking love and Wealtheow's.[101]

The alterity causes an attraction and repulsion, and this becomes intensified due to the attackers' similarities to their victims: both Beowulf and Gardner's Grendel may be seen as more closely allied to these females than they are to any other characters in the works. Beowulf, whose strength seems to have godlike proportions, matches the physical might of Grendel's mother more than any other human. In the novel, Gardner's inversion of this may be seen in the fact that Grendel is the most sensitive and philosophical of monsters, closer to Wealtheow in this respect than any of her own kind. His attraction to her awakens a distinctly vulnerable side to his personality, generally, but also because his outcast state refutes any possibility of his becoming her mate. While she functions as peace-weaver to the humans, she functions as tension-maker for Grendel by

---

[99] Jane Chance, "Grendel's Mother as Epic Anti-Type of the Virgin and Queen," in *Interpretations of Beowulf. Ed.* R. D. Fulk, 1991, Bloomington: Indiana UP: 251-263

[100] (Gardner, *The Construction of Christian Poetry in Old English*, 81)

[101] (Butts, *The Novels of John Gardner*, 94)

exposing his isolation from human counterparts. She is infinitely more kind and giving than the humans Grendel encounters, yet she becomes the bride/wife to his enemy.

As Wealtheow in Chapter Seven of the novel embodies conflicts for Grendel, in *Beowulf* the character of Grendel's mother represents various opposing ideas to the Anglo-Saxons culture. Renee R. Trilling sums up the scores of opposites related to Grendel's mother in the poem: "Grendel's mother signifies the threat of alterity to a closed system, and she becomes a nexus for the many dialectical tensions, male/female, human/monster, hall/wilderness, feud/peace, symbolic/semiotic, that underwrite the system. She reminds society of the parts of itself that it attempts to expunge through abjection, and she represents the continual presence of that alterity, despite its abjection, in an explicitly gendered way. She exposes the inability of language, at its most fundamental levels, to proscribe the limits of gender and agency."[102] On a similar note, Chance states that by disengaging the oppositions, Beowulf attempts to restore order to Hrothgar's world, and by extension to the larger world.[103]

When human models fail, it serves to foil and emphasize the overwhelming power of the protagonist. The female is caught in the tension of balances because of her loyalties. Gardner's remarks on Grendel's mother in the poem, describing her as trapped in a fated role, for he uses these terms, " . . . perverted irascibility of Grendel's dam, whose loyalty is not to Law but to an outlaw."[104] Nor does Gardner fail to recognize the similar aptness of the label "virgin" to Wealtheow, for Chapter Seven states, "But she was beautiful and she surrendered herself with the dignity of a sacrificial virgin" (100). For Grendel in the novel, Wealtheow's loyalty is equally undeserved of the humans, despite the symbols in the text allying even her brother with various heroic motifs: the pet bear on a chain (97), would seem to tie him to Beowulf (as "bear's son"). Similarly, the description of him anticipates a similar description of Beowulf, "His eyes, slanting downward like the eyes of a fish, were expressionless as dried-up wells" (98).

For Grendel, grappling with the Queen sexually and killing the bear both show his supremacy as compared to Hygmod and Unferth. Similar paradigms appear in the poem prior to the second battle, as Beowulf fights

---

[102] Renee R. Trilling, "Beyond Abjection: The Problem with Grendel's Mother Again," (*Parergon* 24.1: 1-20. Project Muse. The Catholic University of America, Washington, D.C. Feb. 2008), 17

[103] (Chance, "Grendel's Mother as Epic Anti-Type of the Virgin and Queen," 256)

[104] (Gardner, *The Construction of Christian Poetry in Old English*, 81)

off the water-monsters as he descends into the lair of the animal-Queen and puts her to death, surrounded by the weapons of the Giants. The sexual tension in the poem caused by Grendel's mother and her role reversal is pictured in Gardner's novel with the inversion of roles at court. Wealtheow is described as carrying the mead bowl at Heorot, her gentle ways affecting the thanes, even Unferth, whom she saves from embarrassment by silencing a verbal attack (102-103). Grendel is touched by her beauty and her kindness and watches her many movements (104-105).

When her brother visits, Grendel is drawn toward the hall by the sounds ("It trembled and shook from the noise inside," 106, an ominous echo and foreshadowing) and he leans against the outside of the building and watches through a crack. "It was the king, old Hrothgar, who carried the mead bowl from table to table tonight. He walked, dignified, from group to group, smiling and filling the drinking cups . . . " (106). This reversal, with Wealtheow in the 'kingly' role and Hrothgar 'as queen,' reflects the inversion in the poem of Grendel's mother as male, both in the poet's pronominal switch, but also as holder of her own hall or dominion.

The chapter ends having established the following criteria: a female causes disruption in the normal flow of events, tensions of alterity mount, the protagonist feels forced into challenging her role and her sexuality and does so, grappling with her in a scene full of erotic terror, and order is restored. The second battle shows the attacker in his full maturity, but also on several fronts as a foreigner to the victim's court. Both vengeance and fealty reflect the opposite poles of virum—and balance is restored on multiple levels. Gardner's Grendel, now fully representative of Cain's clan, wittingly or no, comes to represent as well the forces in humans which transpose innocence to envy, isolation to rebellion.

The first episode concerning the maternal figure shows the disruption of the protagonist's world order that leads to a brutal attack, while in the second episode, the need for vengeance and the restoration of order calls for the attacker to accost the female. The poem as well as the novel set the second episode in the female's territory, wherein the male physically overcomes her in a manner rife with sexuality; he asserts masculine identity through dominance and restores power to his domain. In the poem, Beowulf restores order by going to the lair of Grendel's mother and battling with the monster-inverted-into-Queen to render her back to the role of completely monstrous. In the novel, Grendel restores order in his theoretical (or intellectual) universe by attacking the human-inverted-into-angel and showing her to be merely physical.

Grendel, Chapter Seven, Surveying the Text

After having taken up the mantle of enemy as suggested by the Shaper, promoted by the Dragon, and defined in opposition to Unferth's heroic aspirations, Grendel reaches adulthood near the midpoint of the novel. The novel itself is balanced between Grendel's innocent past and his ferocious legacy, so on a narrative level, one senses in Chapter Seven the start of real mayhem. When we reach the point of Grendel's becoming truly ferocious, the narrative perspective of the novel becomes imbued with the reader's knowledge of events given in the poem, coupled with the Grendel that Gardner has given us in Chapter One, who is at the end of his infamous career.

Gardner achieves a great deal of connotation in a single sentence, and on a variety of textual levels, from the chapter's opening line, "Balance is everything, riding out time like a helmless sheepboat, keel to hellward, mast upreared to prick out heaven's eye" (91). The line recalls the ending of the previous chapter, its "alternative visions of blind old poets and dragons" (90), a rhetorical riddle implying Grendel has found balance. It would seem a good omen except his "keel" is "hellward," and this implies balance between good and evil, though leaning toward hell. This opposition between good and evil is not his own.

The metaphor of this opening introduces many concepts. The boat image anticipates Beowulf's arrival in a boat, which comes as a response to the monstrous attacks on Heorot; the Geat may be said to function as a balance to Grendel's atrocities. The sheep-boat may also be seen as a symbol of female sexuality related to Grendel's mother, with symbolism of the boat as a womb. As well, "sheepboat" signifies Grendel's own state of being as it relates to his mother: "sheep" last figured prominently in Chapter Three, when Grendel described his sense of self as dual (in that instance, an imbalance) and his mother as a "baffled, indifferent ewe" (44).

Simultaneously, however, the image calls to mind masculine sexuality in terms of the old ram in Chapter One who desired to mount anything nearby, including a "spraddle-legged ewe" (6). While this may seem a stretch of inference, consider how the ram represented Hrothgar, "cocks his head like an elderly, slow-witted king," (5), how Hrothgar's "ewe" would be Wealtheow, and how Grendel later in this chapter will pull "her naked legs apart as if to split her" (99). Further, the keel is the most important element of a ship's structure, in this case balanced perpendicularly by the mast. The mast as an "upward prick" is another sexual metaphor, a sign of his adulthood and foreshadowing the nature of the events to follow, in terms of Grendel's attraction to Wealtheow in episode one (and in his assault on her femininity in episode two).

Gardner's analysis of the preliminary to Beowulf's second battle bears note here, "The second movement begins with a curious summary of material from the first movement. The unexpected attack of a second monster prompts the poet to speak again of the first, of Cain's exile, and of Beowulf's victory, and thus allows him to reinforce his meaning by repetition."[105] In the novel, Gardner mirrors this, opening Chapter Seven in the "present action" of the narrative, the twelfth year in his war against Hrothgar.

Concerning balance, Grendel notes his physical supremacy to the Danes but also recognizes how he must hold back his desires in order to maintain the bounty of his human prey. Grendel notes, "My enemies define themselves (as the dragon said) on me. As for myself, I could finish them off in a single night, pull down the great carved beams and crush them . . . " (91) This recalls the brutal descriptions of his raids. The brutality, Grendel asserts, is balanced by his new philosophy concerning "form" and "function" and he asks "What will we call the Hrothgar-Wrecker when Hrothgar has been wrecked?" (91)

In Chapter Seven, Grendel is outraged by the sight of Wealtheow having brought peace to the Danes through her marriage to Hrothgar. In a kind of jealous rage, he attacks her sexually, grappling with her. Wealtheow herself is the image of virum here, for the war with Hygmod's people has been avoided through this union with Hrothgar. At the time of Grendel's attack, these previously warring tribes have come together in the Mead Hall to celebrate their pact. She is also the image of womanhood compromised, both by the marriage to a much older king in order to save her people and by the ravaging Grendel.

A comparison can be made to Grendel's mother as an image of womanhood compromised, both in her relation to Cain and as a female prompted by loyalty to her "people," Grendel. In both stories, a male enters the female's lair where the trappings of past war victories decorate the walls, a physical grappling with sexual overtones ensues, the central point of conflict involves family and loyalty to family, a significant motif is blood, and the attacker is described as one with an ability to grapple (comparable to bears)

---

[105] (Gardner, *The Construction of Christian Poetry in Old English*, 76)

Episode One

The narrative moves back to the past, Episode One begins as Grendel follows along in joyful anticipation of a bloodbath just as Hrothgar's men arrive for a surprise attack on a rival tribe, the Helmings. The superiority of Hrothgar's tribe is clear and the Helmings have no chance of surviving a battle. In an ironic inversion of family loyalty, Hygmod matches Hrothgar's surprise with his own surprise and offers his sister to the aged king: virum in one sense, insofar as it wisely maintains peace and avoids bloodshed, yet in another way, one not lost on Grendel, Hygmod's act is the ultimate disloyalty to his sister. Gardner is careful to show Wealtheow's dignity in the situation, despite her grief at the idea of separation from her family, and she is shown as giving herself freely out of an understanding that her tribe's survival depends on it (100-101).

While the general penchant for human bloodshed, cruelty, and feuding disgusts Grendel, it also thrills him viscerally, perhaps because it intensifies the idea of his moral superiority. However, the barter of Wealtheow for peace signifies the ultimate alignment of the Shaper's "God" with the murderous Danes, and therefore the height of hypocrisy. Further, Wealtheow symbolizes the maternal instinct to protect the family, and in a description which points out the parallels between her and his mother, Grendel notes this: " . . . I listened to my mother move back and forth, a pale shape driven by restlessness and rage at the restlessness and rage she felt in me and could not cure. She would gladly have given her life to end my suffering . . . Who could miss the grim parallel? So the lady below would give, had given, her life to those she loved." (102)

So, too, does Gardner's novel show Wealtheow's peace-weaving as an inversion of Grendel's former love for her. Her symbolic reflection of his childhood idealism and his former desire for fellowship with humans creates a horror for him, a horror magnified perhaps by the fullness of his maturity, his lack of a viable mate, and the transference of her to Hrothgar, his most despised enemy. This is epitomized in the lines where Grendel reflects on his anguish after Wealtheow is first handed over to the aged king, "O monstrous trick against reason—I was afraid I was about to sob. I wanted to smash things, bring down the night with my howl of rage . . . O woe! O wretched violation of sense!" (100-101)

What follows is a kind of spell preventing him from attacking Wealtheow, perhaps a type of love combined with an understanding of her role as similar to his mother's, yet he cannot overcome the tension concerning her symbolic role as peacemaker. The very association between bartered Wealtheow and his own outcast mother emphasizes his blood connection to the outcast kin of Cain. If he is to assume his role as a mature member of Cain's kin, the only role presented to him by the humans (even Unferth, after all, could speak Grendel's language and visited his lair, but did nothing except discuss his own heroism and need to attack the "monster") then Grendel must attempt to undo the apparent peaceful alliance of these kingdoms.

Many correspondences exist between this episode in the novel introducing Wealtheow and the first episode where Grendel's mother appears in the poem. In both novel and poem, the episode preceding the attack on the maternal figure concerns a surprise entrance from a rival tribe, as well as the instinct to defend one's family, followed by a trade that prompts the vengeful retribution to follow. In the novel, the surprise attack is Hrothgar's warriors on the Helmings. It results in a trade of Wealtheow to the attacking tribe, followed by her silent grief as she is separated from the family of her birth.

In the poem, Grendel's mother makes enters Hrothgar's mead hall for the first time as a surprise attack. She has been grieving silently, having been separated from her son by his murder. She displays her own type of dignity; as we find out later, her strength and abilities rival that of her son's, but she does not ravage the mead hall. Instead, she kills a single victim and then retrieves her son's arm from over the mantle. In Jane Chance's assessment of the poem, the depiction of Grendel's mother in two separate incidents reflects the dual inversions of the character. In the first part, Grendel's mother avenges her son, what Chance refers to as an "inversion of the ideal" image of motherhood, as it inverts the passive peacemaking of the human matrons of the poem (such as Wealtheow).[106]

The trade that Grendel's mother makes, killing a human in retribution for her son's death, even as she takes back what is "hers," her son's arm, is a reflection of the Anglo-Saxon codes of retribution. Acker notes, "Through the irruption of a monster, the text projects the anxieties it cannot otherwise adequately voice concerning the inherent weaknesses in the system of feuding and revenge."[107] As well, when Hrothgar and his tribe discover that Grendel's mother has killed Aeschere, his most loyal and beloved thane, their loss is acute. As Gardner describes it, the death of Aeschere reflects the " . . . central importance of vengeance in this movement."

At the same time, just as Wealtheow's trade in the novel places her in the position of protecting her family through her role as a potential mother to Hrothgar's children, Grendel's mother in the poem attacks from the

---

[106] (Jane Chance, "Grendel's Mother as Epic Anti-Type of the Virgin and Queen," 253-254)

[107] Paul Acker, "Horror and the Maternal in *Beowulf*," (PMLA 121: (704-705)

maternal instinct to protect her family. Of this, Gardner says, "Grendel's mother avenges her son, which is a type of virum yet perverted by her unholy state—both of them outcasts—but her loyalty inspired vengeance leads to the murder of the 'most dearly beloved.'"[108] The attack by Grendel's mother on Heorot represents to the society of Hrothgar's court the uncompromising vengeance of the feminine maternal—not in the abstract but in the actual.

Prior to the appearance at the mead hall, Hrothgar and the Danes are certain their problems have ended with Grendel's death, but the incident necessitates the second episode. Noble Beowulf, though he's an outside to their clan, once more takes up the cause of the Danes and fights Grendel's mother in retribution for her murder of Aeschere, as well as to forestall further bloody assaults on the mead hall. Similarly, in the novel the Danes and the Helmings are celebrating together when Grendel bursts in and attacks Wealtheow. It is the opposite of Beowulf's charitable joining with the tribe, yet it symbolizes Grendel's joining with his "own" tribe, or at least the one ascribed to him by the beings (human and inhuman) he has encountered.

Episode Two

Gardner's Grendel, who has become enraged by the complacency of Hrothgar's brutal court, sees the act of political peacemaking in the Wealtheow barter as the ultimate betrayal, of the "real" human penchant for war, of their all-knowing God, and of his own jealous hatred of them. That she, the only "good" human, should save them from themselves he finds nearly impossible to accept. As Craig Stromme states, " . . . she is the closest thing we see to a Christian in Grendel. Shaper brought the Old Testament to the village, but Wealtheow brings the New Testament ideals with her."[109] The second episode of Chapter Seven, Grendel's sexual assault of Wealtheow, raises important questions about Gardner's purposes and, not surprisingly, causes a maelstrom of controversy when the book is taught in public schools.

Gardner's reasons for crafting this passage that has so inflamed critics of the book, given its inflammatory nature and the fact that Grendel and Wealtheow do not so much as meet in the poem, have not received thorough treatment by scholars. No doubt this is partly because, with the exception of some passages in *Mickelsson's Ghosts* (Gardner's last novel),

---

[108] (Gardner, *The Construction of Christian Poetry in Old English*, 76)
[109] (Stromme, "The Twelve Chapters of *Grendel*," 4)

his works are free from overt depictions of a sexual or violent nature. Not one of them contains the type of graphic combination of those found in *Grendel*.

Indeed, *Grendel* has been banned a number of times that are documented, and no doubt countless times "off the record," which, as Ken Donelson describes such situations in "'Filth' and 'Pure Filth' in Our Schools—Censorship of Classroom Books in the Last Ten Years," happens regularly in the United States. He notes that in a single decade, the novel was officially banned six times by school boards. Donelson quotes the specifics from the most respected source on censorship, The American Library Association's "Newsletter on Intellectual Freedom," which reports the particular comments made by the censors to have been as follows, "no educational value," "too violent and graphic . . . " Donelson quotes the newsletter, "A school board president said ten years ago 'We have a duty to the community and we must guard against the use of garbage being passed off as literature.'"[110] A more specific situation is detailed in "Grappling with *Grendel* or What We Did When the Censors Came," wherein Kenneth L. Zeeman describes being a "department chair . . . besieged by reporters" when a citizen appealed to the NCTE with more than the fifty signatures needed to open proceedings and demanded that administrators ban the teaching of the book in his school.[111]

While the attack on Wealtheow is not the only element of the novel with the potential to raise the ire of censors, it stands alone as the most dramatic.[112] One may see in this a progressively creative use of the characters from the poem: the Dragon interpolated from another space and time but not especially surprising in his draconic materialism and cynicism, Unferth's arrival at the cave as an original scene yet his hypocritical claims to heroism consistent with the jealousy of Beowulf he displays in the poem, and now Wealtheow, whose genteel and maternal characteristics Gardner replicates in his novel, though the plot turns infinitely darker with

---

[110] Ken Donelson, "'Filth' and 'Pure Filth' in Our Schools-Censorship of Classroom Books in the Last Ten Years" (The English Journal 86.2, Feb. 1997), 24. 4

[111] Kenneth L. Zeeman, "Grappling with Grendel or What We Did When the Censors Came" (*The English Journal* 86.2 (Feb. 1997), 49.

[112] Even the old ram's sexual arousal in Chapter One is couched in terms somewhat indistinct for younger readers. Indeed, in my experience, college students by and large do not know why the ram, despite Grendel's shouting at him, refuses to move. They may be led to the conclusion through a series of questions related to the season and the description of the ram wanting to "mount" whatever is near, but the language is not familiar enough to them to be obvious.

Grendel's attack. A close examination reveals that Grendel's attack on Wealtheow is not disconnected from the main events of *Beowulf*, but indeed a masterful reinvention and echo of the poem's structure, an ironic and inverted counterpoint to the poem's second battle. Similarities abound in the role of both combatants, the situation, the reason for the contention, as well as the sexually steeped nature of the assault. This correlation between the second episode in these central battles explains, at long last, what had appeared to be Gardner's disconcerting inclusion of a horrific and explicit sexual assault.

While the sexuality in Chapter Seven of the novel is clear, the sexual implications in Beowulf's attack on Grendel's mother are less overt. Much has been written in Anglo Saxon studies on the hero's second battle, including essays related directly to associative links between Grendel's mother and Wealtheow. First, the poem outlines Grendel's genealogy as Cain's kin, yet he is outcast for more than this inheritance of sin, for the problem lies also with his monstrous appearance.[113] For most readers, the horror of the poem's monsters comes from the tension created by their blend of human and inhuman qualities, as Tolkien and others have pointed out.[114]

This becomes especially important when one considers the specific sexual subtexts in Beowulf's second battle, since the foe with whom he grapples is female, humanoid, and unclothed, none of which would have been lost on an Anglo-Saxon audience. While Beowulf chooses to fight Grendel unarmored, so the contest may be fair, he does not hesitate even a little about wearing armor to fight Grendel's mother. As well, while she is female, many have referenced the poet's occasional and surprising use of the male pronoun to describe Grendel's mother as she fights.

Beowulf, then, in confronting this female force inverted into maleness on the level of a male milieu, needs doubly to assert his maleness. Trillig contrasts it to the armor-less battle between Beowulf and Grendel, "His masculinity was not in doubt when he fought Grendel, but his new adversary's very existence qua adversary brings categories of identity into question, and the masculine performance of donning armour reassures us as much as it does Beowulf and the Danes."[115]

As well, linguistic evidence suggests sexual overtones in several of the Anglo-Saxon words used by the poet to describe Grendel and his mother,

---

[113] Note, for instance, that Unferth, who has killed his brothers out of jealousy, remains a functional member of Hrothgar's tribe.
[114] (Tolkien, "*Beowulf*: The Monsters and the Critics," Appendix A)
[115] (Trilling, "Beyond Abjection: The Problem with Grendel's Mother Again," 17-18)

overtones that are generally lost in the poem's translation to modern English. Nicholas K. Kiessling's study provides an enlightening linguistic analysis. He considers the word "*maere*" as applied to Grendel, and notes that while this term is generally rendered as "famous," such a translation should be reconsidered because in most instances it also connotes "glorious," a term not ascribed to the monster. Kiessling proposes "*maere*" with a short versus long diphthong and this translates as "incubus," which he sees as a much more apt description. He states his purposes as twofold, both the linguistic investigation itself and the proposition of Grendel being an "amalgamation" of various types of Medieval beings, of both Southern and Northern influence.

He provides a detailed list of "long diphthong *maere*" and he notes that in all but three instances, two of them in *Beowulf*, the word has a positive connotation. As for *maere* as *incubus*, Kiessling traces the etymological connections between Germanic languages, showing the connotation both of a night sprite and a creature who squeezes or crushes their prey. Such combinations lend well to the etymology of Grendel's name, he points out, a "grinder" and a "crusher" being quite similar. He goes on to point out various instances of the term's use in the eighth century, including Biblical translations, as well as glosses of *maere* showing it as related to "incubus, satyrus, monstrum."

Further, he notes the inherent similarities between incubi as the "offspring of Adam and female spirits" and Grendel as the son of Cain, in terms of Biblical references to Creation. Linguistically, he shows correlations between incubus and lamia, and then lamia with *maere*, and connects this to lamia-type references that include hairiness, an essence of earthliness, and vampirism, all of which could be said to apply to Grendel (as well as his mother): "Grendel and his mother, those demonic amalgams of English, German, Latin, and Scandinavian tradition, possessed traits that were common to all of these creatures. But only the word incubus could adequately describe a monster of Grendel's dark ferociousness and at the same time include many of the concepts suggested by the words striga, lamia, haegtis, and also monstrum, satyrus, pilosus. And the Old English rendition of incubus is, of course, maere."

Concerning the sexual nature of such creatures, Kiessling mentions Augustine's hesitation as to whether such spirits may couple with humans, and he follows this with Aquinas' beliefs in such monsters as sexual beings whose lust was not satisfied in a purely sexual way, but instead was combined with the feelings that come from envy or jealousy. Kiessling connects this to Grendel's jealous raid on the Mead Hall. Associations of night-maere as "nightmare" are twofold, first in the consistent night quality of Grendel's attacks, but with an additional implication being the dream quality associated with a "nightmare." Kiessling prefers instead Scandinavian associations of "mara" (or witch) as a real troll woman and not as a dream, which seems especially apt as a term for Grendel's mother, and would've connected her sexuality to an incubus, for an Anglo-Saxon audience.[116]

Clearly, in both works, the sexuality of the female is physical and natural as well as theoretical and signifying. As Trilling notes, describing Grendel's mother in the poem, " . . . maternity is nothing if not a physical, bodily state; to be a mother is to fulfill the functional destiny of the female body. Her role as mother forces us to focus on her femininity, but not in the abstract; she is a concrete, material, bodily representation."[117] The same is true for Wealtheow in Gardner's novel. In both the poem and the novel, the second attack episode involves the idea of the female as a direct threat to the identity of the attacking male, and so it is fitting for each of these battle scenes to involve attacking the female in her chamber. Symbolically, such an act would serve to correct the oppositions and undo the threat to the norms of the protagonist.

For Grendel, Wealtheow's peacemaking is as disconcerting. Whereas he regularly murders Hrothgar's thanes, or refuses to murder them out of spite, such as Unferth, Wealtheow presents a distinct dilemma; she "saves" the wretched humans from their own brutality, and he must deal with her by bringing her down from this lofty spiritual state—but in the end, he cannot perform the ultimate conquest of her, a rape or a murder, because something of the angel mystique remains with her and this reflects the high ideals ("Mercy!", "Peace!") he has sheltered since his youth. In a similar vein, Gardner inverts the situation and the particulars.

Both works, as concerns this episode, display the tensions as powerful modes of sexuality and status, evoking the contrast through the setting and the signification of male versus female codes. Likewise, in both works, the female's status is linked to her abode, and it becomes symbolic of her domain, which is foreign to the attacking male. Beowulf must travel to the home of Grendel's mother, a den which represents her natural and uncivilized state. As Acker describes this setting: "The abject is thus aligned with marginality . . . To connect this aspect of abjection with the powers of horror in *Beowulf*, we may recall how the murderous Grendel and his mother reside at the edges of the area of socialization centered in the hall (Heorot), beyond the marches and in a mere at the margin of

---

116 Nicholas K. Kiessling, "Grendel: A New Aspect" (*Modern Philology* 65.3, Feb. 1968): 193-197.

117 (Trilling, "Beyond Abjection: The Problem with Grendel's Mother Again," 9)

which even a hunted stag (heorot) must recoil in horror." He goes on to characterize the poem's battle between Beowulf and Grendel's mother as " . . . a complex and evocative moment" partly because of the ironies in the inverted idea of security within the context of one's home, and he adds, "the fight with Grendel's mother takes place in her den, a place devoted to security for the monstrous pair but death and cannibalization for human prey."[118]

As well, in Gardner's novel the assault occurs in Wealtheow's and Hrothgar's bedroom. This, Gardner points out, is within the parameter of Heorot, not separate from it. Prior to this episode, Grendel has made his beastly prowess known to the humans (it is the "second year" of his "raiding," 94); but upon Wealtheow's arrival to Heorot, he finds himself in a type of mental paralysis. Upon the return of Wealtheow's brother Hygmod with his Helmings, the sign of Wealtheow's marriage to Hrothgar making her the peace-weaver who creates unity between the human warbands, Grendel is lured from his cave. He observes their celebration, goes home again, but then returns with vengeance the next night.

Important details in this chapter of Gardner's novel mirror the scenes in the poem after Beowulf has killed Grendel. The celebration at Heorot shows unity between the Geats and the Danes, Wealtheow appears in her role as Hrothgar's Queen, honors are bestowed. As well, after dark when the warriors are sleeping, one of Cain's kin enters the hall under dark of night in protest. Other details are transmuted, but even when they are, Gardner maintains connective threads between his protagonist and the poem's hero. One of these relates to the aforementioned study by Kiessling on the etymology of Grendel's name as "crusher."[119] In reaction to Grendel having stormed in, Hygmod tries to turn the pet bear on him, but Grendel crushes it in a hug and squeezes it to death.

R.W. Chambers traces commonalities between *Beowulf* and folktales, such as Icelandic ballads centered on Biarki and tales such as "Bear's Son." In it, the character known as Bear's Son is comparable to the character Beowulf and has a "bear- like method of hugging his adversary to death," a heritage which, Chambers asserts, would account not only for Beowulf's incredible physical strength but also his propensity for weaponless combat.[120] Gardner was acquainted with Chambers' work, for he notes, "Chambers' study of *Beowulf* shows that, even though we usually cannot tell where the poet found his materials, we can be sure that he borrowed

---

[118] (Acker, "Horror and the Maternal in *Beowulf*," 703-704)
[119] (Kiessling, "Grendel: A New Aspect," 194)
[120] (Chambers, *Beowulf: An Introduction to the Study of the Poem,* 62-67)

heavily."[121] Bertha Phillpotts, another scholar familiar to Gardner, has noted how this bear-hugging quality allies Beowulf with the monsters in the poem: " . . . when he goes out of his way to boast of having hugged to death a human antagonist, the warrior Daeghrefn (11.2506 ff.), he seems to show bear or troll-like attributes . . . "[122] The death of Hygmod's bear from the "hug" connects Grendel (and his name) to Beowulf, just as Beowulf is connected to the folktales of Bear's Son.

After the death of Hygmod's bear, Grendel makes his way through the human stronghold of the mead hall, killing several as he goes along, knocking Unferth aside, past the scenes of his usual raids to enter another area. The placement of the Queen's lair underscores the human warriors' inability to protect her, for neither her birth family nor her new family stand a chance against Grendel, and neither seem to try very hard. Grendel's assault of Wealtheow comes as a consequence of jealousy over her marriage to Hrothgar and envy of the Danes' potential happiness, especially Hrothgar, but it is personal as well.

As for the actual battle between male and female forces in the poem's second battle, Chance argues that the *Beowulf* poet does not hesitate to include sexuality: " . . . Grendel's mother has a monstrous or sexual nature very different from that of a civilized ides. For, during the passage describing their battle, the poet exploits the basic resemblance between sexual intercourse and battle to emphasize the inversion of the feminine role . . . This is achieved in three steps: first, the emphasis upon clutching, grasping, and embracing while they fight; second, the contest for a dominant position astride the other; and third, the use of fingers, knife, or sword to penetrate clothing or the body, the latter always accompanied by the implied figurative kinship between the sword and the phallus and between decapitation and castration."[123]

For the Anglo Saxons, the attack of the monster woman creates all sorts of social problems, as Trilling conveys, and so the monster woman cannot be treated as are other monsters: Beowulf does not bring back her

---

[121] (Gardner, *Construction of the Wakefield Cycle*, 136)

[122] Bertha Phillpotts, "Wyrd and Providence in Anglo-Saxon Thought" (*Interpretations of Beowulf*, ed. Fulk, R.D., Bloomington and Indianapolis: Indiana UP), 9

[123] (Chance, "Grendel's Mother as Epic Anti-Type of the Virgin and Queen," 259-260). 1 have included only the prelude to an argument that Chance provides in detail, with examples from the text and comparisons to sexuality in other Anglo-Saxon writings, including Old English Riddles, such as Riddle Twenty, as well as the sometimes "sadomasochistic" (note 20, 259) references to sexuality found in *Aelfric's Lives of Saints* (258-260). Some scholars disagree with Chance's interpretation, though Gardner would have been aware of it.

head as trophy, but instead brings back Grendel's, because the female monster's head would be a reminder of the oddities in the situation.[124] In Gardner's novel as well, the alterity of the situation causes tension. By using Grendel as protagonist, a monster which cannot be defeated physically until the hero (unnamed in the novel, but clearly Beowulf) arrives, Gardner must create a situation of tension comparable to Beowulf-and-Grendel's-dam involving the emotions and ideas. Just as the Anglo Saxons in the poem are threatened by the violence of the female monster's aggression, in Gardner's novel Grendel (who is immune to weapons and so does not fear violence from humans) is threatened by the overwhelming introduction of emotions Wealtheow has produced in him.

Gardner's discussion of the poem focuses on how the poet begins the second movement reiterating Grendel's exploits, "Like all we have heard before of Grendel, every statement here insists on his character as cosmic outlaw. He was earlier 'hell-counselor,' guilty of 'crimes' and 'sins,' one who warred against 'right' . . . "[125] Similarly, Gardner's novel returns to the descriptions of the monster's cruel bloodlust, as Grendel refers to himself in the third person, "Enough of that! A night for tearing heads off, bathing in blood! Except alas, he has killed his quota for the season" (93).

In *Beowulf*, the poet's repetition of Grendel's atrocities underscores the ironic position of the creature's mother, who by virtue of being his kin has an allegiance, but whose outcast state makes such fealty unfortunate and doomed. As Gardner says of her in the poem, "Grendel's mother is also of the tribe of Cain, but nothing is said of her crimes or sins. She lives in misery in terrible, cold streams because of the deeds of the outlaw Cain, but she is presented not as an enemy of right but as an avenger" (76).

Beowulf kills the monster's mother, while in the novel Grendel assaults the "mother-to-be," whose offspring are meant to solidify connections between two kingdoms. In the poem, Beowulf travels to the monster's "battle lair" to confront her and bring the problem under control (the problem of the male-female alterity, the problem of monster-human alterity) by overcoming the trait most representative of this otherness—the monster woman's incredible strength—so, too, Grendel travels to the peace-weaver's (new) battle hall to confront and bring the problem of the alterity under his dominion, the attraction-repulsion alterity and the angel-animal alterity, and the mother-wife alterity—by overcoming Wealtheow's spirituality and showing her to be an animal, thereby securing his repulsion.

---

[124] (Trilling, "Beyond Abjection: The Problem with Grendel's Mother Again," 18-19)

[125] (Gardner, *The Construction of Christian Poetry in Old English*, 76)

As Leonard Butts states, Grendel's " . . . attack on her is an attempt to 'expose' her, literally and figuratively . . . By spreading the queen's legs for all the world to see, Grendel thinks he has 'revealed' the illusion of her power—she is after all only flesh."[126] At the end of the chapter, he notes that by the memory of his assault on her, and by focusing on images of the blood between her legs, he has "cured" himself. After Grendel decides not to kill her and runs toward his home, he states, "I concentrated on the memory of the ugliness between her legs (bright tears of blood) and laughed as I ran through the heavy snow . . . " (110). Since he continues raiding the mead hall after this, it would seem that the attack functions, specifically, as cure of his attraction to her. This satisfies the chapter's insistence on themes of balance (Libra) as well. The sexual desire Grendel has felt for Wealtheow is balanced by his repulsion.

The blood image coalesces all of these themes, including the poem's second battle. Most immediately, it relates to Wealtheow's womanhood and the maternal function of peace-weaving; her children, borne from sexual intercourse with Grendel's rival Hrothgar, will continue the line of the murderous Danes. By association, the idea of motherhood connects to Grendel's mother. His blood relation to her connects them both to Cain, as well as to the monsters in the cave to whom he seems to be related, adding further stress to the situation. Acker, in discussing Grendel's mother in the poem, references Kristeva's categories of the abject. He links this to Lacan's notions of psychological growth through separation from the mother and applies it to Kristeva's theories on the abject as a powerful symbol of the need to confront tensions between identity and the maternal. Acker notes, "Within such areas of paradox, horror exerts a perverse fascination."[127]

In terms of associative metaphors between the novel and the poem, when Beowulf uses the magical sword crafted by Giants to cut off Grendel's head, it melts because the blood of Grendel's mother (and perhaps the shared blood between she and Grendel). The sexuality in the symbolism of swords and penetration in the poem, as pointed out by Chance, would connect the melting sword with the loss of erection, just as in Gardner's novel when Grendel says that remembering the blood of Wealtheow has quelled his attraction to her.

For Gardner, the challenge must have been to create a scene that would embody for modern audiences what Anglo Saxon audiences would have found in Beowulf's fight with Grendel's mother: assault bathed in erotic

---

[126] (Butts, *The Novels of John Gardner*, 94)
[127] (Acker, "Horror and the Maternal in *Beowulf*," 704)

alterity, violent conquest permeated by horror, and the ironic elation of climax. Simply showing a sexualized grappling between Grendel and Wealtheow it would not have produced the same effect. While the scene in the novel produces shock, recognizing its corollary to Beowulf's second battle provides important information on Gardner's intentions. Yes, Grendel has become a horrible monster at the midpoint of the novel, but Gardner's use of violent sexuality here is neither mere window-dressing, nor is it part of a larger dark joke, for nothing in the attack on Wealtheow is funny, despite Grendel's laughter throughout it. Instead, the novel is Gardner's unflinching, inverted recast of the poem.

Grendel, Chapter Eight, Surveying the Text

Chapter Eight of Grendel concerns Hrothgar's young orphaned nephew, Hrothulf, and his plans to overtake Heorot and his uncle's throne. The astrological sign Scorpio relates most obviously to the boy, whose place in the court makes him an imminent threat, but whose youth and family status would seem to preclude action on the king's part. At the same time, Grendel may also be seen as a scorpion, a smaller version of the Dragon, with less sting, but still effective as a combatant. Grendel follows Hrothulf and the foul-smelling old philosopher Red Horse, widely considered a reference by Gardner to the philosopher George Sorrell.

After several introductory pages in unrhymed verse which is framed like a play (for, Grendel suggests, he followed and watched without being seen), Hrothulf and Red Horse discuss government policy. Red Horse's diction becomes increasingly modern: "police," "domestic/foreign crisis," "tax collectors" (119). There are criticisms of governments and rebellions, for the portrayal of Red Horse is as one half-crazed and looking out for his own good. However, Hrothulf is young and despite the care shown to him by his aunt and uncle, the King and Queen, the political rhetoric is effective. The situation lends itself to a sense of the court as doomed and, by extension, all governments eventually.

Grendel, in his self-contained debates, notes this, along with the human penchant for self-deceit. He describes Wealtheow as she observes her sons sitting with their uncle Hrothulf. All of them are aware of the potential for doom, yet they cannot accept it. He characterizes Hrothgar's knowledge of the doom impending on his tribe, listing Hrothulf as a danger to Hrothgar's sons (the legitimate heirs), Hygmod who will keep peace for Wealtheow's sake only, Ingeld a rising ruler of a neighboring tribe, and Hrothgar's own wealth, a temptation for robbers. In addition, Wealtheow is an emotional trap for Hrothgar, as she represents the limitations of his old age. Grendel turns all of this in his mind in what appears to be empathy for his enemy.

Then, in a surprise address to the audience, his logic begins to take on the logic of the Dragon. This escalates until he takes on the mantle of a god and claims Hrothgar to be his own creation, which is perhaps a variation on the Dragon's argument that Grendel's role as monster improves the humans. Grendel resumes his address to the audience, yet with a rhetorical shift, not merely in the phrase "you may ask," but directly, an accusation, "Enough! Who says I have to defend myself? I'm a machine like you. Like all of you. Blood-lust and rage are my character" (123). The machine metaphor will come again in the final chapters in descriptions of Beowulf, but here I believe it figures as well in a play on the phrase deus ex machina. Beowulf arrives like a god in the machine for Hrothgar, and the inversion would be Grendel's function as deus ex machina. The word "machine" connoting both antiquity and modernity functions well here.

The allegorical associations seem clear enough: Grendel sees himself on the level of a creator and claims he is above judgment. Moreover, his actions, he claims, are a product of his "character" (123). Both of these connect to his kinship with Cain, but in reaching toward the audience of readers he projects Cain outward and the motif is associated with mankind. While it would seem Hrothulf's disloyalty as secretive scorpion will result in the destruction of Hrothgar's line, Grendel's concerns move the allegory to a broader plane. Like Cain, his misery is compounded by loneliness. And once more the loneliness becomes linked to Hrothgar as the chapter ends: "I have thought up a horrible dream to impute to Hrothgar" (123).

The dream is written in poetry, so the chapter ends in the form with which it begins, and it, too, is a riddle of sorts. The setting is Chapter Two's first meeting between Grendel and Hrothgar, and the "dream" seems to be meant to inform Hrothgar of why this tragedy of the monstrous attacks has befallen him. The "black tree with the double-trunk— two trees grown into one—throws up its blurred branches" (124) refers to the spot where Grendel was hanging when the humans first beheld him. The image may also, in silhouette, represent the image of a scorpion, whose barbed tail might be seen as curving upward like a blurred branch from a trunk; the metaphor would correspond nicely to Hrothulf as being from a "different branch" of the family and Hrothulf as eventual displacer of his cousins, the rightful heirs. Extended outward, the branches of the tree would correspond allegorically to the branches of Adam's tree, or Cain and Abel, also here, blurred, and also tied to images of secretive murder and sin.

Since it is followed by the "quick arc flashing sideways" (124), the strike of the axe also lends itself to the dual association of the tree and violence. On the plot level, Grendel seems to be claiming Hrothgar started the feud—so Hrothgar is now paying for his own reckless attack on the vulnerable cub Grendel. The cub Grendel has grown into an attacker in his own rite, just as the cub Hrothulf will grow into a formidable attacker, through envy seeking to displace Hrothgar's heirs—just as Cain displaced Abel. The allegory shows how the Anglo-Saxon systems of paternity and inheritance malfunction due to selfish ambition, but it shows this to be a universal trait as well, inherited just kingdoms or genetic traits are passed down. This explains the "interlocked" aspect, "The two trunks in their infinitesimal dance of growth//Have turned completely around one another, their join//A slowly twisted scar . . . " (124).

Perhaps the two trees represent the fates of Hrothgar and Grendel, whose pain is now intertwined, whose "growth" is inhibited, each by the other. The chapter ends with the line "I will dream it again," offset so that it could be from Hrothgar's mind within the poem-dream or in Grendel's; both are locked into the conflict. So, too, the descendants are simultaneously interlocked and "locked in"—Hrothulf and Hrothgar's sons—as are all of the sons (and daughters) of Adam. In an artistic sense, Grendel himself may be seen as inheriting his role in the novel from his role in the poem: the dream of the *Beowulf* poet becomes a new dream, translated into a new millennium.

Grendel, Chapter Nine, Surveying the Text

Chapter Nine opens with imagery tying it to the last chapter, "December, approaching the year's darkest night, and the only way out of the dream is down and through it. The trees are dead" (125). The dream and the tree imagery recur, yet now Grendel clearly assumes the role of the dreamer. There is the additional element of death in its many symbolic forms, with the traditional seasonal nods to winter and its cold darkness. The tree with its twisted pain of growth finds its parallel in the many dead trees. Gardner reiterates this in the lines pursuant to those, written in lyrical form, "The days are an arrow in a dead man's chest.//Snowlight blinds me, heatless fire; pale, apocalyptic" (125). As Grendel walks through this "apocalyptic" landscape, the natural becomes the unnatural, as he sees the snow angels made by children, " . . . when they rise, [they] leave behind them impressions, mysterious and ominous, of winged creatures" (126).

The angelic imagery deepens with the line, "Something is coming, strange as spring. I am afraid. Standing on an open hill, I imagine muffled footsteps overhead" (126). This opening of the chapter, with its poem-like form, contains building images of stillness, blindness, and death, with the word "dead" repeated four times in this passage. There is as well some hint at the heavenly, in the snow angels made by the children (though contrasted by the fact that Grendel is on his way to the mead hall) and also in the foreshadowing the arrival of a force, as though from some heavenly sphere.

The next passage involves the bowman hunted hart. The riddle Grendel senses as regards the death of the hart appears first in Chapter Five, the Dragon's apocalyptic great destruction of the mead hall mirroring the end of the world, which Gardner has discussed in *The Construction of Christian Poetry in Old English* (62), and quoted previously. Martin Green, as well, notes specific passages in the building of Heorot " . . . in which the poet links the erection of the greatest of mead-halls to the divine act of cosmogony" as well as less specific allusions to Hygelac's Hall. Green continues, "At the same time, the poet intimates the eventual doom of the two halls (both to be destroyed by fire) and thus connects the two halls in their role as microcosmic symbols to the destruction of the world."[128]

As Chapter Nine begins, the hart is slain by an arrow through its heart, while the sound of footsteps predicts Grendel's death; just as the heavens are sending an emissary in the form of the hero who will slay him, the death of the hart equates to the death of Heorot and the eventual doom of the Scyldings, foreshadowed in the last chapter concerning Hrothulf's treachery. Appearing after Chapter Eight's revelation of Hrothulf's disloyal intentions toward the uncle who rescued him from an orphan's lot, here in Chapter Nine the suggestions of earthly disruption broaden.

The apocalyptic imagery signals a more esoteric subtext, extending outward from the mead hall and the current chronology to include mankind in general, even as Red Horse's diction suggested the modern world with its police forces, border issues, and tax collectors. While Grendel has become "wrecker of the mead hall," a greater force in the cosmos makes itself felt via his instincts, or so it would seem from his narration. In the description given here, the notion of the archer and Sagittarius connects the themes of doom to religion and philosophy.

[128] (Green, "Man, Time, and Apocalypse in *The Wanderer*, *The Seafarer*, and *Beowulf*," 291)

Images of time are connected to the death of the hart, which cannot escape its doom and dies, as do all natural creatures.

Grendel next approaches the Danes' place of worship, and the text contains a surprising mixture of pagan and Christian imagery. This corresponds to the passage in *Beowulf* in which people turn to worshiping pagan gods when their faith runs thin (after many years of Grendel's attacks): "This was great misery to the lord of the Scyldings, a breaking of spirit . . . At times they vowed sacrifices as heathen temples, with their words prayed that the soul-slayer would give help for the distress of the people. Such was their custom, the hope of heathens; in their spirits they thought of Hell, they knew not the Ruler, the Judge of Deeds . . . Woe is to him who in terrible trouble must thrust his soul into the fire's embrace, hope for no comfort, not expect change."[129] Wiilliam Whallon, in his discussion of the poem, notes that the sin of the Danes may be in their idol worship. In *Beowulf*, he points out, the minstrel sings of Heorot in phrases drawn from Genesis, and then Grendel begins his attacks, to which the Danes respond (II. 175-183) "by offering vows to idols and a soul-slayer."[130]

In Chapter Nine, Grendel approaches this area with a sense of triumph in having had no supernatural force, positive or negative, thwart him. Religious institutions and their leaders become the topic of his philosophical inner debates, and he remembers how he once knocked over all of their idols, destroying some of them. Certainly, this is another reference to Scyld (at the start of the poem), though also ironic in its association with Grendel as destroying false gods. He notes their response: Hrothgar's community has replaced the idols, though seeming without enthusiasm, as a matter of superstition. As Grendel describes it here, religion becomes a matter of rote duty, whether pagan or not, with the priests as mere emissaries of the dull traditions.

In its way, the novel seems to closely examine the Anglo-Saxon notion of "wyrd" (our word weird comes from this), the forces in the universe that seem to be separate from godly interference. Some scholars equate wyrd with doom, and in many cases they function synonymously, yet it seems to me that doom (dom) connotes endings, while wyrd has associations beyond this, equivalent even to our notions of weird. A person may be doomed as a function of wyrd, but a person (or culture or tribe) may also be rescued by wyrd; in other words, while doom suggests destiny (and one's destiny may be wyrd), wyrd itself connects to notions

---

[129] (Donaldson, translation of *Beowulf*, 6)

[130] William Whallon, "The Christianity of *Beowulf*" (*Modern Philology* Vol. 60, No. 2., Nov. 1962), 86

of surprise and chaos. The fact that we use ‘weird’ in our daily vernacular (while ‘doom,’ not so much) suggests a cultural mindset tuned more toward unexpected results.

One may see this in the novel starting in Chapter Seven, as the apocalyptic images take on different aspects of doom and weird: first, with Grendel’s movement from inaction to attack and the attack itself being a violence of utter destruction (but then his seeming arbitrary or “weird” decision not to kill the Queen); next, this is hinted at in Chapter Eight with Hrothulf and impending doom of Hrothgar’s court and his immediate line of succession, though somehow the boy seems opposed to this; here, recurring with more force in Chapter Nine, as the seeming stillness and sameness of the world feels contradicted by the sense of danger.

The atmosphere remains tense even in the stillness, as Grendel comments on the other characters as being as restless, this night, as he is. Hrothgar and Wealtheow wait, on their backs in bed but with their “eyes open” (129); Hrothulf has “bad dreams” (129); Unferth “sleeps fitfully” (129); even the Shaper “mumbles a few inchoate phrases to someone who is not there” (129). This is followed by an image that widens to include the world, “in the town below me there are no lights left. Overhead, the stars are blanked out by clouds” (129-130).

The only moving creature, the one to break the stillness, arrives at the circle of idols, Ork the priest. Ork is one of the most sincere characters encountered by Grendel, though also seems somewhat insane. Grendel, as though joking, at first pretends to be The Destroyer. The “Destroyer” finds its closest linguistic parallel in *Beowulf* to be soul-slayer and so one can see Grendel here pretending to be a demon. That Ork falls to his knees and addresses him as “O blessed, blessed lord!” (130) does more than suggest a weird conjunction of Judeo-Christian philosophies.

Grendel seems to pursue the dichotomy here, though he claims to be teasing with Ork, and says, “Tell us what you know of the King of the Gods” (131). Ork doesn’t seem to understand the question, so Grendel elaborates, making it clear by both the singularity and the pronominal reference that he refers to the Judeo-Christian God. Ork remains confused, but does his best to give a lengthy explanation. Howell discusses this in depth, “Ork introduces allusions to Whitehead and inspires allusions to Blake . . . When Grendel asks the blind Ork to tell him about the ‘King of the Gods,’ Ork echoes Whitehead, just as the dragon did. The dragon had mocked the Shaper’s presentation of a connected universe by quoting Whitehead’s *Modes of Thought* out of context. Ork, ostensibly senile, seems equally unreliable when he defines the idea of God using phrases from two of Whitehead's best-known works."[131]

At first, it seems Grendel will amuse himself by violently killing Ork, but as the scene continues, the old priest's genuine faith seems to move him. Again, while doom seems to be operating here, it is attended by weird decisions. Possibly, Gardner means for us to see the human application of monstrosity onto Grendel as one that precipitates their own doom, while at the same time Grendel's awkward resistance to the role brings in the elements of wyrd. Here, Grendel backs away as the other priests enter. Their scene is given in the form of a play, and they reflect modes of dealing with religious attitudes and the public. The First Priest wants the law to be followed, and he chastises Ork for breaking it. The Second is full of compassion for the Brotherhood and sees Ork as one of their own, while the Third is cranky enough to suggest "If a man hankers for visions, he should do it in public, where it does us some good" (134). A younger priest joins them, whom Grendel deems to be drunk, but who lauds Ork as having achieved greatness with his vision. The others look to him as they would "a wounded snake" (136).

The new religion of the younger priest, with its wildness and bodily fluids, calls Dionysian revelries to mind, but within it, despite its claim for "hope," one recognizes this as a call to salvation which has no relation to Judaism or Christianity. If the Shaper's songs of Creation and Cain and Abel were meant to inspire the people to the new religion, Grendel's observations here would seem to prove otherwise, at least for the priests. A kind of ironic perversity appears: Grendel adopts the Cain's kin identity and begins raiding when in fact no one in the town actually subscribes to religious beliefs and, it seems, even the priests themselves have returned to paganism. The suggestion in *Beowulf* is that the hard years of Grendel's murderous raiding have pushed the people to return to their pagan roots; in the novel, this becomes curiously circular. As an apocalyptic image, the discrepancies in religious thoughts and practices, creating a kind of religious anarchy, work well on even the basic level: Grendel the mead hall wrecker pretends to be the Devil, and is worshipped by the "eldest and wisest" (130) priest.

This lack of spirituality within the auspices of a dead world heightens the tension, despite the stillness. As the world waits, Grendel returns once more to the catalog of waiting characters, then to the sleeping animals. The final image in the chapter contains parallels of the type Gardner called

---

[131] (Howell, *Understanding John Gardner*, 74-77)

circular (or mystical) allegory when discussing *Beowulf*: "I do not usually raid in the winter, when the world is a corpse. I would be wiser to be curled up, asleep like a bear, in my cave. My heart moves slowly, like freezing water, and I cannot clearly recall the smell of blood. And yet I am restless. I would fall, if I could, through time and space to the dragon. I cannot" (137).

The bear symbol connects Grendel to Beowulf, and the dragon foreshadows his fight with Beowulf-as-dragon, mirroring Beowulf's fight with the dragon. This predicts the following image which echoes the Dragon's vision of the end of the world: "I recall something. A void boundless in a nether sky. I hang by the twisted roots of an oak, looking down into immensity. Vastly far away, I see the sun, black but shining, and slowly revolving around it are three spiders . . . It is just some dream . . . " (137)

Here again, the allegory is circular, lending to the apocalyptic theme. Grendel cannot recall the smell of blood but does recall the image of lasting death which echoes the speech given by the dragon of a dead sun. With this image comes a return to his childhood in memory, hanging from the tree and looking down, which may be a crucifixion metaphor, but certainly calls to mind his first meeting with humans. Thus, a dream ends both Chapters Eight and Nine as the novel waits for its penultimate, fated meeting between the monster-hero and the hero-monster.

Following the second battle of Chapter Seven, eight and nine serve as digressions, similar to the digressions in *Beowulf* and reflecting them in some ways, though also reflecting Gardner's comments on the modern world. In Chapter Eight, the paternal order of succession is mirrored in the failure of all governments and the depravity of rebellions as well. Chapter Nine suggests that whatever religion the Danes have, it is essentially without connection to the supernatural (at best) and is used as a means of securing power with the public (at worst). As for Grendel, he searches for God but cannot see the signs in front of him, even when he makes himself into a god-figure, which he finds outcasts him further yet.

Apocalypse and Doom in *Grendel* and *Beowulf*

Symbols such as the bear forge allegorical connections between the characters of Beowulf and Grendel, and while these heighten the irony of the monster as hero, irony is neither the only nor the principal effect. Images of the apocalypse begin to enter the poem as Beowulf's second battle ends, a signal from the poet that even a hero at his most dominant stage of life will eventually succumb to death, as God has deemed it since the Fall of Man. Similarly, at the midpoint of the novel Gardner shows Grendel at his most heinous in the attack on Wealtheow, with Grendel at the height of his monstrous identity. In this inverted epic with a godless monster as narrator, the very notion of "apocalypse," removed from the tenets of religion, becomes connected instead to the modern world, the failures of society and its eventual downfall.

Gardner pairs this with Grendel's growing preoccupation with the events of the kingdom, just as in the poem Beowulf's first battle seems designed to establish his role as a hero, while the second and third concern his position within social orders once he's been proven. To see the poem as a chronicle of a hero's journey from youth to death, is to see the novel as an inverted counterpoint. I would argue against letting the matter rest on such notions. The thematic relationship between Beowulf's journey and the Fall of Man (and along with this the links between Beowulf and Christ the Savior), enhance the poem's resonance. To see Gardner's novel as merely a parody of this or a negation of its themes is to disregard the work's fundamental connection to modernism, by which I mean not only "modern life," but also the literary movement of modernism.

While Howell treats Grendel as a viable protagonist, likening him to Gardner's Fred Clumly from *The Sunlight Dialogues* and noting the novel's connection to Coleridge and Blake, he calls the novel " . . . a work of metafiction," and an "improvisation and parody" in which " . . . Gardner deconstructs the original epic's characters and actions (and many of its lines) by placing them in an ironic context which implicitly questions the vision of the original work while saluting its literary power . . . "[132] All of these can be true, even as one takes those ideas several steps forward. If one sees Gardner writing the novel as an homage to the original, but using the themes and events to solidly ground his protagonist in modernism, the significance of the work rises significantly.

In chapters seven, eight, and nine, Gardner begins to show Grendel's impending doom as directly resulting from society's mistreatment of him. Certainly, Grendel makes choices leading to his downfall, yet to limit him to a static role as the 'ironic anti-hero' is to deny the character his true place as one of the most powerful outcasts in modern literature. If one takes Grendel's evolution toward doom seriously, aside from the brutal tone and the moments of parody, one finds a deeply rooted study of alienation and madness. While Howell sees Grendel allied with Gardner's Fred Clumly, I see a much closer correspondence to Pete Mickelsson. Both Mickelsson and Grendel are philosophers who pivot between

---

[132] (Howell, *Understanding John Gardner*, 61-62)

madness and doubt, who find themselves shuttled toward doom by a society they disrespect but can't ignore (try as they might), yet they are characters whose vulnerabilities attract us, despite ourselves.

The novel may be metafiction and parody, but more importantly, it is as well an allegory to the Fall of (Modern) Man that parallels the doom of the Danes (a culture rescued briefly by a hero just as it was tortured by a monster). By extension, it becomes a metaphor implying the eventual demise of mankind, or at least the innate tendencies for ill-fated personal destiny, depending on the level of one's existentialist leanings. Grendel's personal apocalypse will reflect broadly, and extend outward in this second half of the book, even as it pauses its movement toward the death of Grendel. Chapters Eight and Nine, following the attack on Wealtheow corresponding to the poem's second battle (Beowulf killing Grendel's mother), anticipate the final battle and the death of the protagonist in both works. It is fitting then, like the poem, for the novel to use digressions in order to reflect on the wider base of human community and institutions. These digressions contain apocalyptic images, as does the poem, because both works anticipate and foreshadow death.

In the interview with Bellamy, Gardner commented on this section of the novel: "At about Chapter 8 there is a section where you are no longer advancing the momentum toward the end . . . We have now developed the whole position of Grendel, you know; it jells when Grendel meets the dragon. At this point, nothing more happens to Grendel. He's just waiting to meet Beowulf—it's just the wheels spinning. That is not novelistic form; it's lyrical form."[133] Just prior to this statement, Gardner calls this one of "a number of problems in Grendel." Bellamy has challenged Gardner's claim that modern novelists are indifferent to form.

This "wheels spinning," while it does not advance the plot in terms of Grendel's future, connects his destiny in a "lyrical" way to the humans. Here, Gardner unleashes some of his most stinging criticisms of society, showing, in fact, not only how communities exile the so-called monstrous and create their own enemies but indeed how individuals consistently deceive others for personal gain. Worse, they are self-deceivers. In Chapter Eight, even though Hrothulf has been graciously taken in and raised by his Uncle Hrothgar and Aunt Wealtheow, he plots their destruction. Red Horse the philosopher knows it and tries to call it what it is. In Chapter Nine, while Ork is second only to Wealtheow in his goodness, his fellow priests reveal the complete hypocrisy of their religious institution.

---

[133] (Bellamy interview, *Conversations with John Gardner*, 21)

Still, along with the criticisms, these passages do show in humans an underlying tendency to want goodness, to aim for some sort of truth; it is as though Wealtheow's introduction to the kingdom allowed this new perspective, either in the humans generally or in Grendel's altered view. Or, perhaps Grendel has established his identity and can now see the vulnerabilities in people, as shown in characters new to the story such as Hrothulf and Ork, but also in the principal players such as Hrothgar and the Shaper. It is, however, tempered by the rising undercurrent theme of society as damned, and so even as individuals show the desire for truth, they are limited by their egos and cannot reach beyond their wants.

In these chapters of digression, as Grendel sneaks from tree to tree and spies on his human counterparts, the signs of disaster mount. They apply equally to humanity (as typified by its institutions) and to the monster's outcast state. The elements of apocalyptic literature enhance the feeling of doom while connecting ever-monstrous Grendel to humankind. In an allegory of the Fall of Man, if Adam and Eve are considered first generation, and Cain and Abel second generation, then Grendel may be seen as the third-plus generation. With him are the Danes who have inspired his monstrous evolution and on whose social models he has fashioned his personal destiny.

Perhaps the most difficult task in writing such a novel, based as it is on a poem concerned with man's place in the cosmological scheme chiefly as it pertains to God's judgment, comes in how to locate such notions within the inverted lexis of alterity within a modern framework. Each of these chapters concerns tension between natural and unnatural/supernatural, and a focus on the role of the divine in human (and monsters') affairs. From the outset, the issue of alterity has kept Grendel separate from his human counterparts, with the direct result being his philosophical debates questioning the existence of God. In his search for identity, Grendel spins his own web of reality, yet it remains undisciplined and unconfirmed due to his isolation. Certainly, the Dragon figures into this paradigm, as did the Dragon in *Beowulf* and the serpent in the tale of the Garden, all symbols of prideful greed.

Empowered with superhuman strength, the desire for companionship, and a natural capacity for submission to leadership, Grendel has attributes which would have made him the most superior of thanes were it not for his otherness. This otherness includes a shocking outward appearance (when they find him in the tree, Chapter Two, they cannot identify his species), the inability to speak so humans can understand, and the tendency toward rage. As a matter of course, Hrothgar and the humans preclude him from participation in society. Yet more than this, they confer on him a heinous new identity as hell daemon, offspring of Cain, outcast unquestionably and from birth. Although he seems to scoff at the significance of the Shaper's Biblical references, the issue resurfaces when he feels exiled: "A glorious moment was coming, my chest insisted, and even the fact that I myself would have no part in it—a member of the race God cursed, according to the Shaper's tale—was trifling" (108).

Having been outcast, Grendel takes the role offered him and makes himself into a self-created god, eventually seeing himself as an antidote to the very notion of God, "I would kill her and teach them reality. Grendel the truth-teacher, phantasm-tester!" (110) This identity as may call Satan to mind, yet Grendel is not Satan, even in the metaphorical sense; he struggles for an apprehension of truth, he suffers, and he longs for community even as he perpetrates evil, none of which apply remotely even to the Dragon. Grendel's anger comes from his lack of a viable connection to any reference point outside of himself, including his mother, natural and supernatural creatures, humans, and God.

When neither reasoning nor supplication fashions bonds, his loneliness and jealousy manifest in violence; this murderous spite associates him with Cain. In Chapters One through Seven, the link to Cain functioned on a level of identity for Grendel, but as the novel progresses past its midpoint, the broader topic concerns the allegorical implications of such kinship. Nor are such connections absent from the poem. For the poet, calling Grendel "Cain's kin" defines the general status of exiles insofar as their place outside of human community reflects their disassociation from the Divine; similarly, the closer one draws to God, the more important one's place becomes in society.

The description does much more than this. Indeed, it functions as a tight, symbolic parallel between virtue and sin, showing all men to be capable of (if not prone toward) falling from grace. According to Goldsmith, "The spiritual sons of Cain are all those who 'build their cities' in this world, like Hrothgar at Heorot, pinning all their hope on a false good." Indeed, she says, " . . . old King Beowulf's struggle with the dragon, who as the shape of the devil typifies pride, and as *goldweard* typifies covetousness" is "the realization of what Hrothgar's warning has foreshadowed."[134] Even good Beowulf, sent by God to end Hrothgar's trouble, will be tempted, and will, at least in part, fail.

Nor is the symbolism of the monsters reflective merely of values, but are meshed within chronological, allegorical, and associative links. As

---

134 M.E. Goldsmith, "Christian Perspective in Beowulf," (Comparative Literature 14.1, Winter 1962), 79

Goldsmith states, Hrothgar's suffering prior to Beowulf's arrival, and the decline of his clan even after Beowulf vanquishes the monsters and departs, may be seen as the result of pride, which places a boundary between man and God. "Slowly, the darker side of Heorot is revealed: it is to be destroyed, and the Scylding line cut off, through the workings of envy and murderous hatred within it. These are the sins of the generation of Cain, embodied in the destructive beast Grendel and his dam." Goldsmith sees Grendel's role in the poem, therefore, as an incarnation of that which exists already in the humans, such as is revealed in their world activities. This in itself links the Scyldings to their monster enemies.[135]

Acker's contextual view on this differs somewhat: "The reader of *Beowulf* may be struck by how Grendel and his mother are not introduced into the narrative so much as they materialize within it. Grendel first appears after the description of the building of Heorot and the subsequent forecast of its destruction by fire once sword-hate ("ecghete" 84) has been awakened . . . he emerges . . . as if stepping out of the smoke which will envelop Heorot; he materializes from the prospects of failure that haunt all human endeavors, all attempts to build a stronghold of socialization in the wilderness."[136]

In both cases, a direct correlation exists between the horror which is Grendel and the human struggle to balance desire for achievement with a moral life. Gardner was familiar with Goldsmith's article and cites it in a footnote.[137] For Gardner's novel, told from the outcast's perspective, the identity Grendel adopts as Cain's kin and "phantasm-tester!" becomes a refutation of Judeo-Christian notions of goodness through humility. Finding no likeness of such virtues in men, he eschews their hypocrisy, especially since they exclude him automatically. Likewise, the Teutonic ideal of strength used for service of the clan cannot be realized by Grendel. Nonetheless, he struggles to secure a creed or a clan, but cannot.

The root of his problems, his absolute aloneness, persists even in the face of the frantic business of the human world around him. How can one have a clan without an extended family or any memory of ancestral kinship? How can one adopt a viable creed when the society and its accepted religious codes are hypocritical? And even if one could see beyond this hypocrisy, what if society itself precludes one's admission? Such questions in a modern context are recognizable to most readers, indeed perhaps more so than the conflicts which test Hrothgar and

[135] (Goldsmith, "Christian Perspective in *Beowulf*," 74)

[136] (Acker, "Horror and the Maternal in *Beowulf*," 704)

[137] (Gardner, *The Construction of Christian Poetry in Old English*, 134)

Beowulf. Yet, considering the value the world of Hrothgar's court placed on physical prowess, how much more rejected Grendel must feel.

At this point in the novel, the implications of a larger allegory become actualized. The identity of Grendel as Cain's heir, foisted upon him by humans whose connection to the divine is equally suspect (at least in the novel), creates an allegory of the apocalypse, or what many Christians believe will be the final fall (and resurrection) of man. As M.B. McNamee points out, *Beowulf's* Grendel is himself a symbol of man's fallen state: "The human situation of a race fallen from grace is hinted at, too, in the fact that Grendel is represented as a monstrous offspring of the murderer Cain."[138] However, Gardner's Grendel is innocent of wrongdoing until his first attack on the mead hall. Indeed, the first "murder" with which he is associated (in Chapter Four) was perpetrated by humans on humans, and mistakenly attributed to Grendel. In the poem, Cain's having murdered his brother becomes associated with Grendel and his mother, as kin. In the novel, this association shifts from the so-called monsters to the humans.

I have had students remark that this shows Gardner's lack of regard for the "original story," meaning *Beowulf.* Yet in the version of the story with which most Christians are familiar (via the Old Testament of the Bible), there are no monsters to take the blame (except Satan, by extension), so as far as the "original story," one could see Gardner revisiting it by placing man's doom back in the human domain. The humans in the novel resemble Cain, the unwitting heir to Adam's fall. Jealous, brutal, and lacking mercy, they are no longer in connection with the Divine except as a device for passing judgment on others; their hypocrisy locks them into self-blindness.

Chapters Eight and Nine reveal this in the larger sense. While an apocalyptic reading of *Beowulf* is not typical of the scholarship, Martin Green makes an intriguing analysis. Concerning the imagery, he notes its parallels to symbols associated with the fall of man.[139] He refers to Frank Kermode's literature as connected to deep levels of consciousness because our humanity forces us to consider the meaning of our beginnings and our endings. Green links Kermode's statement to the following useful definition of the apocalyptic in literature, "The dominant concern of apocalypse is, obviously, the end of the world and the natural and man-made cataclysms to occur at the end of days; its most familiar imagery is

---

[138] M.B. McNamee, "*Beowulf*—An Allegory of Salvation?" (*Interpretations of Beowulf.* Ed. R.D.Fulk. Indiana UP), 90

[139] Martin Green, "Man, Time, and Apocalypse in *The Wanderer*, *The Seafarer*, and *Beowulf*" (*Old English Shorter Poems*, ed. Katherine O'Brien O'Keeffe, New York: Garland Publishing), 280

the horror and terror of a world dislocated and doomed—the perturbations of the natural world, the decay of society, the disruption of human relationships, the multiplication of evil, and the loosing of demons, spirits, and monsters into the world of men—the signs and portents which the apocalyptic writers insisted must precede the intercession of a divine agent into the flow of time."[140]

Further, scholars have remarked on the combination of historical accounts uniting the past with the present and foreshadowing the future events of the poem. Shane Waller in his introduction to *Beowulf* states that the poem's Germanic traditions are juxtaposed with references to legends, and, as well " . . . the elegiac tone and the sense of wyrd (fate) are so dominant . . . that the poem maintains a compelling unity . . . " (iii). Green sees this unity of time as one indication of its "historical consciousness," and likewise says " . . . The Germanic history and legend interlaced throughout the narrative is but one sign of this consciousness; the allusions to Scriptural history in the poem provide an even larger historical framework against which (or in the midst of which) Beowulf is seen in action."[141] Edward L. Risden in *Beasts of Time, Apocalyptic Beowulf* draws similar conclusions, and makes special note of Gardner's novel, "Gardner in his novel Grendel mentions Apocalypse three times, and this fiery if flawed story seems constantly on the verge of exploding in a violent end."[142]

Gardner's other works contain references to the apocalypse. David Cowart remarks that Gardner's use of symbols suggestive of The Book of Revelation was not limited to *Grendel*. He comments on what he considers overly done apocalyptic symbolism in *Smugglers*, the parody pop-fiction novel in *October Light*, in which on doomsday the smugglers end up on the island known as Lost Souls Rock. Cowart points out how in the interior novel, just before the earth is obliterated, a flying saucer arrives to save them and the smugglers gaze up to it with all the reverence of the chosen people witnessing the Second Coming.[143] As with Smugglers, Grendel contains structural affinities to apocalyptic themes, as well as making the occasional joke about them.

---

[140] Frank Kermode, as qtd. in Green (*Man, Time, and Apocalypse in The Wanderer, The Seafarer, and Beowulf*), 282-284

[141] Shane Waller, *Beowulf: Introduction* (London: Dover Publications), iii, 291

[142] Edward L. Risden, *Beasts of Time: Apocalyptic Beowulf* (New York: Peter Lang), 11

[143] (Cowart, *Arches & Light*, 127)

Despite Gardner's characterization of this section as "spinning,"[144] the sense of doom creates its own momentum. Leonard Butts states, "With Gardner's careful manipulation, the pull of the first-person narrative working on us and the pull of entropy that Grendel feels become one, moving inexorably toward Grendel's death."[145] Even as Grendel's own doom approaches, Chapters Eight and Nine concern his observation of the failure in human social systems: apocalyptic images proliferate. Moreover, such deceit is fostered by the very institutions at society's core: government, family, religion, and ceremony. Indeed, Grendel shows the human race so thoroughly grounded in greed that its own systems will not be able to save it from disintegration. It is here that one finds Gardner's establishment of a moral structure going beyond the parameters of both his novel and the poem. Through the use of apocalyptic imagery, Gardner turns Grendel's story from the inverted reinvention of an Anglo-Saxon poem into a modern allegory about redemption and doom, about identity and salvation.

Scholarship on *Beowulf*: Who (What) are the Monsters?

One of the earlier interests of *Beowulf* studies concerns how one should perceive the monsters in the poem. The question of the species or racial identity of Grendel and his mother, as seen in the poem, has been covered broadly by *Beowulf* scholars, principally because while the two attacks on the mead hall categorize them as monsters, the poet gives them several human qualities as well, when their lives intersect with the mead hall. Perhaps the most famous widely anthologized of such essays is J.R.R. Tolkien's "The Monsters and the Critics."[146] Tolkien has been considered the scholar who saved the poem from disapprobation at a time when many others felt the work to be inferior. He argues against the view of Grendel and his mother as purely symbolic creatures, and indeed asserts the importance of their relation to the human race. Tolkien was inclined to classify the two of them as human-like, and he saw in the poem a progression from this to the more "elemental" form of life (the dragon), fitting his view of the poem as heroic elegy.

In Appendix A of the essay (Grendel's Titles), Tolkien makes a linguistic analysis of terms applied to *Beowulf's* first monster. "As an image of man estranged from God, he [Grendel] is called not only by all names applicable to ordinary men, as wer, rinc, guma, maga, but he is

[144] (Bellamy interview, 21)
[145] (Butts, *The Novels of John Gardner*, 88)
[146] (Tolkien, "*Beowulf*: The Monsters and the Critics," 243-296)

conceived as having a spirit, other than his body, that will be punished." Despite Grendel's association with devils and Hell based on the connection to mankind's sin (and evidenced by his behavior, outcast state, and attitudes), Tolkien does not consider Grendel to be a devil, per se but, indeed, to be a creature with a soul like those in men.

More specifically, he claims, the poem deals with the monsters not as commonplace representations of Hell's demons, suggested by R.W. Chambers.[147] Rather, Tolkien describes the *Beowulf* poet as one who " . . . was still dealing with the great temporal tragedy, and not yet writing an allegorical homily in verse. Grendel inhabits the visible world and eats the flesh and blood of men; he enters their houses by doors." Investigations of the poem's form and content suggest the need to consider closely the classification of the protagonists and antagonists as well as their parallels to outward models. Gardner's own scholarship on Fulgentius expresses this desire to decipher the poet's influences and apply such models to the structure of the poem.

Accordingly, if, as Gardner sees the poem, Beowulf and Grendel both display arma (with Grendel's arma as perverse), then in some sense the heroes and the monsters are operating under similar cosmic influences. Further, for Gardner as well as for Tolkien and others, importance is placed on the fact of both hero and monster as active participants in human events whose choices validate or violate codes of human behavior. While the choices may be relative to symbolic functions of the characters, the very notion of choice privileges individuality. Such a shift does not negate the importance of allegoric connections, yet it does modify the emphasis of inquiry, as it opens important questions concerning the individual identity of the protagonists.

Concerning Grendel's and his mother's classifications, the critical inquiries of earlier *Beowulf* scholars often favored more figurative definitions. Most of the early analysis centered not on the human qualities of Grendel and his mother but on the broader, symbolic relevance of the monsters to the poem's themes. Published twenty years after Gardner's death, Johann Koberl's *The Indeterminacy of Beowulf* provides a convenient overview of the body of *Beowulf* scholarship, the majority of which Gardner was certainly acquainted (as shown in his references within *The Construction of Christian Poetry in Old English*).[148] Koberl covers the history of the critical perspectives as well as providing a framework for a

147 Chambers, R.W. (*Beowulf: An Introduction to the Study of the Poem*. Cambridge: Cambridge UP, 1963)
148 Johann Koberl, *The Indeterminacy of Beowulf* (Lanham: Univ. Press of America, 2002)

comparison of them. His starting point, his own childhood confusion concerning the "unhappy ending" of Beowulf's death by dragon underscores his general thesis about the poem's ambiguities and its probable influences.

This is not to say he finds the poem inaccessible or disorganized; on the contrary, the book well expresses the sturdiness of the poem's central structure while seeking answers to the dilemmas it contains (among them, Beowulf's death). While Gardner would have certainly argued with any suggestions by Koberl of the poem's possible multiple authors, nonetheless Koberl's primary critical mode for such inquiry resides in attempts to establish frameworks for the poem's themes, and, in essence, to uncover its core. Koberl, in this spirit, recounts the history of symbolic analysis and comments on the monsters' context within these perspectives.

Concerning such delineations of Grendel and his mother, Koberl outlines the following categories: Mullenhoff's seasonal/mythical approach, with Beowulf as Freyr and Grendel and his mother as springtime floods of the North Sea (35); Beowulf as Thor and Grendel as "swamp or malaria" (36); Grendel as Beowulf's "shadow self" (37), a foreshadowing of Freud; Christian approaches with Beowulf as Old Testament hero/representation of Yahweh, and with Grendel and his mother as personifications of Cain and the other evil giants (41); folktale approaches, with Beowulf as Bear's Son and Grendel as one of the many bogies of the North (46); myth as history, with Grendel as "personification of enemy tribes . . . sea raiders . . . and subjugated nations" (46); psychological approaches, with the "monsters representative of human weakness"; Christian allegory with Beowulf as Christ and Grendel as Satan and/or the monsters of darkness (74-75); political allegory with Beowulf as Germania and Grendel as the Roman legions (76); as counterpoint opponent to Beowulf, transforming Heorot into Hell just as Beowulf enters the mere and transforms it into Heorot through victory (125-126); as guest/gaest of Hrothgar and the ambiguities of such a title (146-148). As well, Koberl provides commentary on Grendel's human versus inhuman attributes within these categories. Koberl favors the "shadow self, psychological metaphor," and sees this as encoded within several of the symbolic delineations above.

The idea of the monsters as primarily metaphoric, as such was represented in the works of Mullenhoff and others, came under scrutiny by William Witherle Lawrence's *Beowulf and Epic Tradition*.[149] Gardner notes, in *The Construction of Christian Poetry in Old English*, referencing

[149] William Witherle Lawrence, *Beowulf and Epic Tradition* (New York: Hafner, 1967)

the familiarity of the *Beowulf* poet with the Aeneid, "Many critics . . . have worked on the problem, but our knowledge stands where W.W. Lawrence left it . . . "[150] Lawrence points against a mythological or allegorical assessment of the poem. He asserts that arguments by scholars such as Mullenhoff and Klaeber assume the poem to have been structured around a total framework, with such a framework underpinning an allegory; both Mullenhoff and Klaeber note the importance of the three battles fought by Beowulf, and use this tripartite sequence to connect the poem to nature and seasonal myths.[151]

Lawrence, on the other hand, shows the logic in comparing the poem to folktales (as does Chambers). He cites many examples of stories that include a "hero fighting first a monster and then the monster's mother," and he likewise notes the plentitude of "hero fighting dragon" stories.

Further, Lawrence relies upon Panzer's earlier work on the categorization of *Beowulf* within folktale motifs. He notes, "Over two hundred variants of the marchen that underlies the Grendel episodes were listed, and others have since been noted" (171). Indeed, Lawrence uses these motifs and the cultural differences to explain some of the seeming anomalies of the poem. For instance, while many readers of the poem have wondered at Beowulf's apparent lack of loyalty to his men when he watches Grendel enter the mead hall and kill the closest warrior, an act which would seem contrary to Germanic notions of warrior loyalty, Lawrence gives a satisfactory explanation based on the marchen tales. In several versions of similar folktales, the "Beowulf character is younger and less experienced than his companions and must, out of respect, let them first have a chance at the monster" (176). In referencing Grettis Saga, Lawrence states that a "comparison . . . shows clearly what kind of monsters the Scandinavians conceived the Grendel kin to be . . . " (179), including suggestions of waterfall trolls, ghosts, and bears.

R.W. Chambers in *Beowulf: An Introduction to the Study of the Poem*[152] (which Gardner references a number of times in *The Construction of Christian Poetry in Old English*), discusses Lawrence and argues for an interpretation of *Beowulf* as derivative from a common source and related to Scandinavian folk tales. This position counters earlier scholarship on the poem as mythological and allegorical. "Is it not far more easy to regard the story of the fight between Beowulf and Grendel merely as a fairy tale, glorified into an epic?" (47) Chambers shows parallels between Beowulf's fights with Grendel and Dam to the Grettis Saga (48), including similarities

[150] (Gardner, *The Construction of Christian Poetry in Old English*, 130n2)
[151] (Lawrence, *Beowulf and Epic Tradition*, 164)
[152] (Chambers, *Beowulf: An Introduction to the Study of the Poem*)

such as a cliff/underwater setting, the wrenching off of the monster's arm, a magical sword found on the wall, the bloodied water suggesting the hero's death, and so on. While some have suggested one work as derivative of the other, Chambers posits it more likely that "both come from one common source" (51).

He goes on to trace commonalities to other folktales, such as Icelandic ballads centered on Biarki (57-60), and tales such as "Bear's Son" (62-65). In this tale, Bear's Son, comparable to Beowulf in some respects, has a "bear-like method of hugging his adversary to death"[153] (65-66), a heritage which, Chambers asserts, would account not only for Beowulf's incredible physical strength but also his propensity for weaponless combat. Chambers' work is extremely useful in several respects. His thorough treatment of the folktales includes complete renditions of them (in original languages and in translation, 147-195). As well, in supporting his contention concerning the poem's source, he examines the "Cain" paternity, which relocates such Scandinavian monsters from waterfalls to fens and moors (186-187). This explains, he notes, the seeming contradictions and confusions over the setting of Grendel and his mother's abode.

Chambers gives an impressive etymology of the places in England that contain the word "Grendel" or some derivation thereof, including pits, becks, meres, and gates (304-321). Chambers as well gives a history of the scholarship, noting Lawrence as the first (1909) to argue against "the mythological interpretation which allegorized Beowulf's fight with Grendel and Grendel's mother into the struggle of god against the hostile powers of nature" (451). Then Panzer, according to Chambers, discusses Beowulf in relation to Bear's Son and many other folktales (451-452). Lawrence next (1913) brings in the possible connections to Grettis Saga and the idea of the Grendels' cave area as once being set in a waterfall location. Chambers uses this history to further his own arguments about many of these works coming from a common source. This movement from allegorical assessment to folktale analysis shifted the focus on Grendel and his mother from external symbols to functions of the plot—in essence, from monsters who symbolized conflicts wider than the plot, to monsters as a test of human strength or weakness, as folktales normally represent them.

Tolkien brought both ideas together while arguing for the poem's coherence and brilliance. In essence, he credits the poet with integrating Northern sentiments and pagan tales with Christian ideologies, using

---

[153] Note the connection to Gardner's *Grendel* Chapter Seven, where Grendel hugs Hygmod's bear to death, making Grendel, in effect, a "Beowulf."

symbolism from both to create fully realized characters.[154] Gardner, in *The Construction of Christian Poetry in Old English*, lauds Tolkien's praise for the *Beowulf* poet, and, while he mentions Tolkien's allowance for possible discrepancies in the poem, quotes Tolkien, " . . . no proof of composite authorship nor even of incompetent authorship."[155] In addition, more than had previous scholars, Tolkien posits the importance of Grendel's (and this mother's) humanness. His listing of the Anglo Saxon titles given Grendel (in Appendix A), and his close etymological scrutiny of terms, opened new ways of exploring the poem.

The etymological approach grew in favor among critics. By contrast to those who see the signs of Grendel's monstrous nature as inherent in the physical descriptions of him, Signe M. Carlson proposes that folklorists and literary scholars have "invented" the monstrosity of Beowulf's foes. Carlson takes the idea of the original poem's corruption to a new level, not only proposing all Christian material to have been added by scribes, but also suggesting the first author meant for his audience to take the creatures in the poem as literal, if somewhat exaggerated, portrayals of real-world phenomena; folklorists and translators, he maintains, have corrupted this vision. While in part this may sound similar to Tolkien's theories on the monsters as "real" monsters, Carlson means actual real-world phenomena. The evidence he provides for these claims is less than compelling in places, especially his "real world" dragon, a large reptile whose "flame breathing" he believes to have been a representation of a reptile's flicking tongue.[156]

Still, the linguistic elements explored by Carlson make for interesting study. For instance, the use of gaest or *geist* in translation (as either "guest" or "spirit") creates a very different notion of a creature's natural properties. Similarly, Carlson notes *feond* as either "enemy" or "fiend," and again, the translation of "fiend" connotes supernatural aspects. Further, he notes how "*zoncf*" (hand) is variously translated as "claw" or "talon," when referring to Grendel (362), a prejudice on the part of translators that creates an unknowing prejudice among readers. At any rate, the linguistic study bears note, as does the notion of subjectivity in translating, with texts changing through time as a result of such layers.

Nor has more recent *Beowulf* scholarship ignored the question of Grendel. Andy Orchard's 1995 *Pride and Prodigies: Studies in the Monsters of the Beowulf-Manuscript* compares several works in the manuscript in

---

[154] (Tolkien, "*Beowulf*: The Monsters and the Critics," Appendix A)

[155] (Gardner, *The Construction of Christian Poetry in Old English*,131n21)

[156] Signe M. Carlson, "The Monsters of *Beowulf*: Creations of Literary Scholars," (*The Journal of American Folklore* 80.318, Oct. 1967), 357-364

terms of their monsters (*The Passion of Saint Christopher*, *The Wonders of the East*, *The Letter of Alexander to Aristotle*, *Beowulf*, and *Judith*) and seeks connections between them based on the themes of pride and prodigies.[157]

Concerning Grendel, Orchard notes the human aspects inherent in Hrothgar's initial description of Grendel and his mother, suggesting that even the inhuman aspects (Grendel's size, alienation) show him to be a different type of human, and not a beast (31). Later, Orchard discusses Grendel and his mother's abode, comparing it to the Otherworld and connecting this to descriptions of Grendel relating to demons, the devil, and hell (39). Yet here as well, Grendel's humanity is stressed by the original authors.

In Chapter Three, Orchard performs a close study of the poem's treatment of Grendel as Cain's relative, in particular pointing out the concepts of being marked, of wandering off into the wastelands, and of being separated from other men at a point in time. This proposes the conjecture of a type of sympathy engendered toward Grendel (ideas Orchard revisits in *A Critical Companion to Beowulf*, 2003). Orchard points to the poet's development of Grendel in the poem, not as monster or "other," but as a man doomed by an inherited curse, a distinctly human condition.

The Biblical scholarship here is useful, not only in its close rendering of the text, but in its explication of Christian tradition—for instance, in the linking of Heremod to Grendel (63), as well as the idea of Christian abhorrence to Grendel's cannibalism and blood-drinking (64). Such theories suggest Grendel as more monstrous due to his affiliation with humankind, rather than more monstrous due to his otherness. "The consumption of blood is a feature which links not only Grendel and the antediluvian giants, all of whom can in some sense be said to come from the kin of Cain, but it is also an essential part of Cain's own story, and is given as a prime reason for God's curse (Genesis IV.II)" (65).

Yet Orchard does not dispense with the definition of Grendel as a monster. To the contrary, he makes interesting observations on possible connections between the Liber monstrorum and *Beowulf* (110-112, and qts. Whitbread "The Liber monstrorum and *Beowulf*," 465). Most especially fascinating are the similarities in descriptions of certain monsters to Grendel and his mother, including oddly flaming eyes and the propensity for their blood to melt iron.

---

[157]Andy Orchard, *Pride and Prodigies: Studies in the Monsters of the Beowulf-Manuscript* (Cambridge: D.S. Brewer, 1995), 25-9

In Chapter Six, "Grettir and Grendel Again," Orchard provides a comparison outline of events, and notes the previous scholarship on the topic (140-151); he points out that Grettir, in the scene depicting the end of his life, has been compared to both Beowulf and Grendel (158), and concludes the chapter with the notion of similar qualities in the stories. Orchard ends with how such comparisons show closely linked associations between the world of men and that of monsters, and further states that perhaps the strongest similarity between Beowulf and Grettir are their abilities to cross between such worlds (168).

Similar lines of reasoning may be found in Orchard's more recent work, *A Critical Companion to Beowulf* (2003). Orchard here largely focuses on the means by which the *Beowulf* poet infuses the monsters with human qualities or, at least in subtext, and creates structural motifs binding them to concepts familiar to human culture. He asserts, " . . . the poet appears through verbal repetition to cause thematic links to be made across the narrative, and in this case the effect of the repetition is for distinctions between the worlds of monsters and men to become blurred" (64). Thematic repetition in the poem, as outlined by Orchard, includes information that Hrothgar ruled for fifty years before Grendel attacked him; Grendel's mother has ruled the fens for fifty years before Beowulf attacks and kills her son; and Beowulf rules for fifty years before his battle with the dragon (63-64). Similarly, Orchard notes that Grendel is described as a man (*wer*) and as a ruler of his territory.

Later, Orchard shows how the poet evokes sympathy for the monsters through word choice and contrast. Grendel, for instance, enters the mead hall and has "never faced a harsher fate" (lines 718-719, as qtd. in Orchard 192). As well, Orchard states, the poet not only mentions the mourning of Grendel's mother as a motivation for her attack, but uses the opportunity to draw sympathy from the reader by contrasting this sorrow to the joyous festivities of Heorot (193). Orchard gives a close reading to the battle scenes, comparing Grendel's to his mother's attack on the hall, noting the length and characterization given each (192-202), paying special attention to how the poet informs us of the monster's "perceiving" and "beholding" Beowulf.

Such choice of words, Orchard suggests, urge the listener not only to interpret the monsters as those with human-like perceptions, but to participate with them in their struggles (196). The close parallel of descriptions further connects Beowulf to the monsters, in Grendel and Beowulf both being described as "guests" in the mead hall and in the symbolic parallel of Grendel and his mother having skins mostly resistant to weapons just as Beowulf's mail shirt makes his skin impenetrable (197-198).

Gardner, therefore, may be seen as pursuing such ideas in his recasting of the poem. His structural patterning of the novel may be seen as a continuation of the paradigms within the original. Gardner's scholarship on *Beowulf*, centered as it is the Fulgentian scheme in its overall arrangement, shows his interest in structural parallels as well as his belief in the artistic sophistication of the poet. He observes the importance of Christian motifs within the poem, and notes the significance of Germanic values within the community, all while pointing out how the ideas of Fulgentius function to unify these ideas.

For example, the symbolism of the mead hall has of course been inverted and also extended: what stood, before, for the macrocosm now stands for the microcosm as well. As the hall is guarded (e.g., by Hrothgar), a man is guarded by his rational part. As the hall may be attacked by a monster (e.g., by Grendel) when the guardian trusts too much in himself (cf. 1769 ff.), a man may be overcome by pride, an effect of the irascible and concupiscent souls' tyranny over the rational. Hrothgar, of course, fares better in the analogy than Heremod. His trust in God's justice and control brings Beowulf to aid the Danes (*The Construction of Christian Poetry in Old English* 65-66).

With the poem's parameters in mind, Gardner concocts a creature both connected to the human species and distinct. The human ancestry is inferred by Grendel at several junctures, as it is in the poem "Unhappy creature, he lived for a time in the home of the monsters' race, after God had condemned them as kin of Cain" (Donaldson, 5). Yet, Grendel is isolated from humanity, " . . . he who dwelt in darkness" and " . . . known as a rover of the borders."

One may fairly assume in the poem, as in the novel, he is equally isolated from natural creatures by his self-awareness and self-consciousness. In the novel, Gardner highlights this by repeatedly describing animals as going about their daily rituals with a sense of purpose and contentment, if not always by logic (as in the case of the ram).

CHAPTER FOUR

BATTLE THREE: DRAGONS & REDEMPTION

Grendel, Chapter Ten, Surveying the Text

Chapter Ten begins with a series of statements connecting what has happened with what is to come, linked with images of destruction bound in stagnation, starting with "Tedium is the worst pain" (138). The "dull victim" of tedium stares at "seasons that never were meant to be observed." This suggests a warped sense of averted doom, as though Grendel feels he should not have survived his intentions to kill himself. Perhaps this relates to the dragon's charm on him, a supernatural intervention which lengthened his life miserably. Next, "The sun walks mindlessly overhead," a return to the black sun-apocalypse image ending the last chapter, only here as the personification of a mindless god, echo of a descriptions in former chapters.[158]

It is as though Grendel's foray into being a god has left him without even the appreciation of adrenaline brought on by thoughts of an apocalypse. Next, Grendel thinks of the young priest who preaches about the gods and joy, but the people are not paying attention, even in the most basic ways. While this may give the impression of Grendel's philosophical rationalism, in the denial of the supernatural, in the next moment Grendel seems to smell the dragon or sense his presence in the world. A declarative phrase which ends this list "The Shaper is sick," (139) surprises us and also foretells the end of an epoch.

It is for Grendel as though these three separate ideas follow in logical order, the hypocrisy of religion, the existence of supernatural entities, and the end to the artist who first represented those ideas for him. The end of art creates its own artistic moment in the traditional funeral given the Shaper: nothing comes from any of this, in Grendel's view, attendant to his tedium. When Chapter Ten ends the time of the Shaper, Grendel's own

---

[158] "The sun spins mindlessly overhead. The shadows lengthen and shorten as if by plan," Chapter One (7).

time has come to an end, yet he refuses to acknowledge it, even though his mother, whose instincts have been shown to be true, feels the death sentence.

This prelude to the third battle reflects Beowulf's situation prior to the final battle in the poem. As the end of his long (successful) reign draws near, Beowulf's kingdom is threatened by a force fundamentally different from any he has faced before. Tolkien describes Beowulf's "doomed resistance" to the monsters in the poem, and here we may see Grendel in the novel affecting a stance of resistance. Just as Beowulf's first two battles showed his triumph on the material plane, in proving his worth as a warrior, Grendel's first two battles in the novel show him asserting his identity as separate from human definitions (even as, ironically, he fulfills them); here, prior to the third battle, he reports the signs suggesting cosmic forces at work.

While in the first two battles his identity was forming, like Beowulf in the time period before his third battle, Grendel becomes aware that life on earth is fleeting. The monster who has slain so many for so long finds himself unable or unwilling to continue in the role, even as the moment of his own death seems to approach. Tolkien's comment about Beowulf fighting the dragon, quoted earlier, seems now to apply to the monster Grendel in Gardner's novel, "The placing of the dragon is inevitable: a man can but die on his death-day."[159]

In the novel, the image of a goat follows the zodiac sign Capricorn, and in its use and placement at the end of the chapter, it alludes to the Shaper himself (and his illness), as the ram alluded to Hrothgar, in Chapter One. Structurally, this concurs as Grendel has now returned almost to the time at which the novel opened. Just as the goat will die and the Shaper will die, Grendel's death approaches. Unlike the ram incident, where Grendel shouted and shook his fists at the indiscretion of natural creatures, here Grendel attacks the goat viciously, stoning it to death, and the description is both vivid and gruesome. The shaggy comic cartoon Grendel who turned puddles to ice with his ferocity is now reified as a beast that batters creatures to death.[160]

Here, we see a trick in time achieved by Gardner's narrative, for this is the same Grendel with whom we started on page one, at nearly the same moment in time, except now we have experienced through flashback his

---

[159] (Tolkien, "*Beowulf*: The Monsters and the Critics," 286)

[160] Grendel's violent killing of the goat may be Gardner's nod toward the first digression in *Beowulf* when the hero returns home to Geatland after killing Grendel and his mother: Queen Modthryth is known for torturing those in her kingdom who offend her even a little.

progression from innocence to depravity. This allows an appreciation of Grendel's suffering endured. At the same time, it serves as reminder of the intense pain and suffering caused by his violence, in both the human world and the animal kingdom. We also see more closely his descent into madness, in the rapid switch from one mood to the next. What follows is an odd conglomeration that once again highlights his inability to perceive of himself as humans would see him, even after twelve years of raiding.

Grendel watches the activity of the human world at twilight, in poetically lyrical description. The next passage is evocative of Grimm's fairy tales, an old woman telling children a story. Grendel perceives the woman to be lying because she tells of a monster-giant who looms over children, children who "should" listen to their mothers and come in (as in the 'old wives tale' warning of the bogey-man). Ironically, he does not believe the story of the giant, though in fact he himself is a creature out of the nightmares of folklore.

Some may see this is an indication of Grendel lacking an imagination, yet his descriptions and metaphors show creativity and a vivid imagination. What he lacks, in fact, is the keen perspective of oneself as a being in the world. Nor can he rely on his animal instincts for help him avoid danger. In the cave, Grendel's mother seems to intuit some disruption in nature, but he fails to regard it.

Despite having crafted an identity from the Shaper's songs, and having adopting notions of his own godhood from his physical dominance over humans, he cannot see the possibilities of his own downfall, even though the foreboding signs suggest it, even at the deathbed of the Shaper. In this deathbed scene, Gardner brings forth many of the novel's characters, only seen in a new light. For example, Wealtheow and Hrothgar attend with their children and Hrothulf holding hands, polite and waiting as the Shaper dies, even though we know from Chapter Eight what the nephew plans for the kingdom.[161] The Shaper's death ends the epoch, but what is coming may be worse than an ending.

The suggestion of time confluence, the convergence of past and future into the electrified present also attends apocalyptic themes. Accordingly, Grendel thinks of the intangibility of the past, "Not only ancient history— the mythical age of the brothers' feud— but my own history one second ago, has vanished utterly, dropped out of existence. King Scyld's great

[161] Similar to the chapter's possible connection to the Modthryth digression earlier, the tableau of Hrothgar's children holding hands mirrors a digression made by Beowulf upon his return to Geatland. He tells the Geats of the engagement of Hrothgar's daughter Freawaru to the Heathobard Ingeld, and suggests this arrangement will produce feuding and death for the Danes.

deeds do not exist 'back there' in Time" (146). Bringing in the past, even to negate its existence nonetheless vivifies it. At the funeral itself, Grendel sees the apprentice Shaper, the new bard who will, presumably, craft the *Beowulf* poem from the lays of the old Shaper and the events to come (or some of them). The young shaper sings the song of Hengest and Finn (148), a tale of waiting and then retribution and ultimate vengeance, a tale which foreshadows Hrothulf (as did Chapter Eight), in terms of the fate of Heorot. In a more important way, the digression foreshadows Grendel's death, as does the appearance of the new Shaper.

Grendel ends the funeral scene with the words, "End of an epoch, I could tell the king. We're on our own again. Abandoned" (149). As the epoch ends and Grendel tries to make sense of the words his mother says, a single phrase seems to hang in the air: "Beware the fish." This heralds the approach of the hero, the end of Grendel's own reign as Hrothgar's nemesis. Nutter says, "The Christian symbolism of the Fish as Christ, a symbol of rebirth at the end of the zodiacal cycle as the seasons turn toward renascent life, is not lost on Gardner."[162]

As well, this ending resembles sections of the poem concerning King Hygelac's death and funeral; the young son of Hygelac and questions of his ascension parallel the young Shaper's appearance at the old Shaper's funeral. In both the novel and the poem, a dragon figure will appear to challenge (and kill) our protagonist. Thus it follows that just prior to the end of Chapter Ten, the Dragon appears, albeit figuratively, "Scent of the dragon" but certainly as an influence on Grendel's thoughts, "A stupid business. Nihil ex nihilo, I always say" (150). Yet something does come from all of this: the novel has promised the destruction and deconstruction of society, ending its epoch, and a showdown is on its way. So it is that Gardner sets the stage for Beowulf's arrival and the third, final battle in both the poem and the novel.

Grendel, Chapter Eleven, Surveying the Text

In several important ways, Chapters Eleven and Twelve resemble the *Beowulf* poem more closely than any other section of the novel. This makes sense, as the poem's prelude to Beowulf's arrival, his landing on the shore of the Danes, and his fight with Grendel are literal one-on-one correlations of time and place to these scenes in the novel. They are figurative ones as well, as Grendel's final battle patterned the poem's deadly fight between Beowulf and the dragon. At the same time, however,

[162] (Nutter, *A Dream of Peace*, 74)

these episodes are completely distinct from the poem. Gardner's use of allegory and his inversion of the poem's particulars create a narrative closely centered on individual suffering rather than on aligning oneself with the will of a divine entity. It is, after all, in the modern tradition of protagonists with psychological wounds whose society alienates them, rather than a Medieval poem about salvation coming by way of an epic hero. As well, the novel's application of apocalyptic motifs raises the reader's sense of doom. Yet salvation exists here, or so Gardner has claimed, and since the allegorical motifs coalesce the notion of Grendel as the universal descendant of Cain with Grendel as a contemporary outcast (if not a modern "everyman"), there are certainly possibilities for broadly applicable life affirming themes, despite the approaching death of our protagonist.

Chapter Eleven opens with the sentence, "I am mad with joy" (167). This, Grendel's response to the arrival of the Beowulf and the Geats, shows him to be perhaps afraid for his life, perhaps looking forward to the end of his misery, but certainly eager for the vitality of a fight. Risden, speaking of the notion of time and immortality in relation to the apocalyptic heroism in the poem *Beowulf*, says "The death wish and the life wish correspond, and their exhilarating meeting in the apocalyptic moment creates the center of gravity . . . "[163] This is true of *Grendel* as well.

The description of the Geat ship itself contrasts Grendel's metaphor of himself as a ship in Chapter Seven, yet here we have the sense of destiny as providence, at least for the Geats, " . . . the icebergs parted as if gently pushed back by enormous hands, and the ship sailed through, sea-eager, foamy- necked, white sails riding the swan-road, flying like a bird!" (151). This passage clearly mimics the passage in *Beowulf*, "Then over the sea-waves, blown by the wind, the foam-necked boat traveled, most like a bird . . . They thanked God that the wave-way had been easy for them."[164] The changes Gardner makes are noteworthy: the parting of the icebergs, as simile, emphasizes the nature of the divine in bringing the warriors as quasi-natural, as quite large in scope and coming from above, as well as allowing for Grendel's disbelief with "as if" (151), which mirrors his former similes "as if by plan."

Yet the "plan" here starts to resemble a master plan, in that the descriptive "as if" suggests a positive, a distinct change from Grendel's earlier views. Here, it looks *as if* there has been an intervention, whereas

[163] (Risden, *Beasts of Time: Apocalyptic Beowulf*, 8)

[164] (Donaldson, *trans*., *Beowulf*, 7)

formerly these ideas were qualified by the negative: then, although it looked *as if* the natural world moved via a plan, Grendel always appended such a statement with a description of the sun (or moon, or stars) as "mindless." As well, while at the start of Chapter Seven, Grendel provided a metaphor of himself as the "helmless" sheepboat (with its phallic and rebellious mast), here Beowulf's boat is notable for its white sails which, with the divine intervention of the shifting icebergs, help it to "fly." The description also brings to mind the astrological sign for this chapter, Aquarius the Water-Bearer. In this case, the hero is "water borne" and the bearer would seem to be the boat itself and, by extension, the divine presence which bears the boat safely through the waters.

After witnessing the interaction between Beowulf's men and the coast guardian, Grendel stirs "in his cave" (151), a recall of the bear metaphor, though signaling here the end of a long hibernation. He compares this to the quasi-spiritual motivation he felt when pulled toward the presence of the Dragon in Chapter Five. He hears (or imagines he hears) footsteps overhead (152). While he rationalizes this as his own heartbeat, he nonetheless associates the sound with the arrival of Fate, and suggests the inevitability of the moment. Grendel's association of blood with kinship on one level makes this a recognition of his position as Cain's kin (doomed), as well as combining with his general pairing of blood with the life-blood and vitality or blood loss and death.

Along similar lines, on the arrival of Beowulf and his men, Grendel begins describing the world with words that connote associations to death, via paleness, colorlessness, and a repetition of neutral-colored grayness, suggesting, perhaps, that a connection to spiritual forces is also a movement away from all that is natural to blood-filled creatures. Perhaps as well, paleness connotes a supreme strength, impervious to death, the opposite of Grendel's notions of death as a blood-bath, death as the spilling of life's blood. This metaphor of grayness recurs through the end of the book, and calls to mind Grendel's use of the color throughout the novel: in Chapter One, the old woman Grendel kills has iron-gray hair, in Chapter Two, the firesnakes are "gray as old ashes," and the humans have "gray-white faces," in Chapter Five, a hundred pages earlier, "I was half prepared . . . to see God, bearded and gray as geometry, scowling down at me, shaking a bloodless finger" (53). Here in Chapter Eleven, the natural world itself begins to replicate the color gray, as though it also feels the effects of the hero's arrival, "Lead-gray water sucked quietly . . . at icy gray boulders. Gray wind teased lifeless trees . . . the cry of a gannet, invisible in grayness above me" (152).

The sunlight blinds Grendel as it reflects on their armor, echoing the blinding snow equated to the apocalypse in preceding chapters (155). He is at the height of his career at Hrothgar's court—he is the self-termed "Grendel, Ruiner of Mead Halls, Wrecker of Kings." Yet, too, we see him at the end of his time on earth, bored to the point of suicide, and feeling sheer joy at the possibility of engaging with worthy opponents and perhaps at the possibility of his own death. When he watches the approach of Beowulf (who is never named in the novel) and the Geat retainers, he notices the gleaming of their armor with a kind of lust—the first time he has shown any emotion except disgust toward armament. He will face a foe stronger than any he has faced before, and in his attempt to maintain his reputation, he dies.

Nor is strength Beowulf's only attribute as given here, but he has a nearly inhuman aspect as well. To use Tolkien's description of the dragon in the poem, the Beowulf at the end of the novel seems "elemental." Grendel describes the hero and his men as "mechanical," which calls to mind his first encounter with men in Chapter Two, but here the size and strength of them (they are "big as trees"), is paired with death: " . . . quick as wolves—but mechanical, terrible—the strangers leaped down . . . never speaking, walking dead men . . . " and "They moved like one creature, huge strange machine." (155)

This intensifies as Beowulf himself is described. Grendel seems to see him as a being wholly separate from humans (and other mammals who display their vigor through animated sounds and movements): "Voice of a dead thing, calm as dry sticks and ice when the wind blows." His mouth is described as moving "independent of his words" (155). The danger Grendel feels is coupled with a new excitement and aliveness, in an odd contrast to the unnatural stillness. Further, Grendel begins to associate Beowulf with snakes, "The eyes slanted downward, never blinking, unfeeling as a snake's," calling to mind the Dragon, and then with fish, symbolically linking him to Christ, "He had no more beard than a fish." (152-154). This resonates from the previous chapter and the warning that came as if from a vision, or perhaps from his mother, "Beware the fish."

On the return to his lair, the cave once more becomes a metaphor for Grendel as a bear, but also for something deeper, connected to the passage of time and also timelessness, the sense of space as infinite yet also limited and confining, Grendel as a part of nature and so part of the timelessness but also, as a creature of nature, fated to die within his time span. Beyond these thoughts, he wanders past philosophical trails inspired by other characters or his own observations (156-158), and even considers staying still and safe until the Geats depart.

This moment of altruism lessens somewhat as the stranger and Unferth trade barbs about the swimming contest with Brecca. The scene is altered little from the poem, except Grendel in his narration adds more ominous details of description—the stranger's lips seem to be "not moving" when he talks (163); his eyes are seen as "pits" (161). Gradually, Grendel becomes more and more involved with the mechanical calmness of the hero, his machine-like qualities, and it makes Grendel seem the more human by comparison. Even Grendel's vulnerabilities and fears make him a sympathetic character compared to Beowulf.

As the chapter draws to a close, Grendel states, "It is the business of rams to be rams and goats to be goats, the business of Shaper's to sing and of kings to rule. The stranger waits on, patient as a grave-mound. I too wait, whispering, whispering, mad like him. Time grows, obeying its mechanics, like all of us" (165). The suggestion seems to be an acceptance of Fate, if it follows that a monster's business is to be monstrous and a hero's business to vanquish monsters.

Time figures in here, along with the progression of the zodiac. The sign of the ram which started the cycle and drew to a close when the Shaper died in last chapter's sign of the goat, here becomes fulfilled in the water-bearer image. Aquarius the water-bearer brings Beowulf to the land of the Danes, and perhaps as a Eucharistic image of Christ and the cup of salvation, Beowulf bears a cup of "water" to Hrothgar's court, symbol of salvation on the earthly plane, salvation from the monster plaguing them. This will lead into the sign of the fish, Pisces, and Grendel's fatal end.

Beowulf, as hero, greatly contrasts the humans. Is his non-living appearance a manifestation of his higher moral values or is it indicative of a divine state, a being separated from the world of earthly desires and foibles, of blood and sperm? Should we see him as the ultimate proof of Grendel's warped view, or as evidence of mankind's inner cold-blooded nature, an inability to feel what others feel? Clearly, for Grendel he represents Death, but that still doesn't answer the question. The chapter ends with the words, "The Geats build up a fire, prepare to sleep. And now, silence. Darkness. It is time" (166).

Grendel, Chapter Twelve, Surveying the Text

The last chapter of the novel pairs with the zodiac's last sign, Pisces the Fish. We arrive at the penultimate third battle in the novel, Grendel's fatal fight with the poem's hero. The novel has circled back to its beginning, which was also the poem's beginning, yet here at the novel's ending we have as well the final parallel of the three battles, Beowulf's fight with the dragon. The timelines merge in a complex and somewhat confusing way; while the novel has circled back to its beginning near the end of Grendel's life, which happens near the start of the poem, this chapter of the novel also reflects the end of the poem and the death of Beowulf, with attending mirroring images and themes.

In Chapter Twelve, Beowulf the hero of the humans now seems to become, in Grendel's eyes, a dragon. Of course, in the structural scheme of Gardner patterning Grendel's three battles on the poem's, this stands to reason. Several important correlations exist here to the poem and Beowulf's last encounter, his fight with the dragon. First, and most obvious, both Beowulf in the poem and Grendel in the novel will face the biggest challenge of their lives and battle to the death. More importantly perhaps, both do so willingly, for unlike Grendel in the poem, Gardner's protagonist in the novel knows full well what he is getting himself into as he enters the mead hall for the last time. Even so, he enters Heorot and breaks its silence as he tears down the mead hall door, "swollen with excitement, bloodlust and joy . . . " (167). This bloodlust mirrors the unmitigated greed of the dragons in both the poem and the novel. Grendel attacks, kills, and eats the first victim after having put on a napkin to enjoy the feast.

When he grabs Beowulf, the hero makes a transition from machine-like (emphasized in the previous chapters of the novel) to dragon. At first, the descriptions are comparative in nature, " . . . his hand still closed like a dragon's jaw on mine" (168), and "his crushing fingers are charged like fangs with poison." (168). Then, the hero suddenly sprouts "fiery wings" (169, 172), and he "breathes fire" (170). Indeed, Beowulf's manifestation as a dragon operates on multiple levels. On the plot level, it calls to mind the Dragon from Chapter Five. This is no accident, for when Beowulf begins to whisper, Grendel hears some of Dragon's exact lines, for instance, "A meaningless swirl in the stream of time . . . " (170).

This creates complications in terms of seeing the novel's Beowulf as a paragon of virtue. In Chapter Five, the Dragon's high appraisal of treasure-seeking is portrayed as the antithesis of beliefs of God's existence. After refuting the existence of God and the need for morality, advocating instead a positive need for monstrosity as a defining force, the Dragon scoffs at Grendel's questions about God: "What god? Where? Life-force, you mean? The principle of process? God as the history of Chance?" Gardner, discussing the poem, equates the dragon's treasure with moral failures, evidence of the Fulgentian primus gone awry, "And thus, fittingly, the dragon's hoard is the legacy of a dead race."[165]

Many have questioned Beowulf's becoming dragon-like in this last chapter of the novel, not only in its seeming connection to the Dragon in Chapter five, but in Beowulf-as-dragon's abject cruelty to Grendel. In making Grendel sing about walls (another reference to Sartre), Beowulf demands that Grendel "feel the wall" (171) and then he "smashes" Grendel against it, a move that "breaks open" his forehead. Next, he makes Grendel sing, howl about the hardness of the wall, and then whispers at Grendel, "'Terrible . . . Terrible'" and he "laughs and lets out fire" (171); the laughing continues even as he tears off Grendel's arm. While the actions would seem to replicate those in the poem, Beowulf's commentary here and his seeming to toy with Grendel differ quite a bit from the hero of the poem in this same circumstance.

Howell suggests that Beowulf-as-Dragon is a projection of Grendel's own internal evil self onto the hero (70). This explains the cruelty in Beowulf's attack and is consistent with Howell's analysis of the Dragon in Chapter Five as a psychological projection. In this, Howell provides a possible reading of the novel's ending: "Grendel has become his own Shaper, and when he shakes his head against the illusion of the dragon he sees an unmediated reality, and returns to a paradoxical innocence born of the contraries of faith and doubt. Feeling at one with the universe, Grendel asks himself 'Is it joy that I feel?' In doing so, he discovers the only spiritual redemption that Gardner, like Blake, consistently affirmed."[166]

Other scholars approach it differently. Morris locates *Grendel* within Gardner's scholarly approaches to *Beowulf.* Morris works out in some detail Gardner's theories on the three virtues and how they may correspond to moral elements in *Grendel.* For Morris, these elements are reflected in character studies within the novel, with Hrothgar, the Dragon, and Grendel each in some way distorted and inverted images of the three distinct ideals. Morris asserts correlations between Gardner's medieval scholarship and elements of the novel, and he sees the tripartite soul concept in *Grendel* as bound to a character framework drawn on moral lines. Morris uses this to build a case for the novel within a moral construct. He sees Gardner as praising an exemplified tripartite soul in the Shaper, Unferth, and Beowulf, while showing the inverted and negative tripartite soul via characterizations of Hrothgar, the dragon and Grendel. Given this, Morris has no objection to the actions of Beowulf in Chapter Twelve, and

---

165 (Gardner, *The Construction of Christian Poetry in Old English*, 81)

166 (Howell, *Understanding John Gardner*, 88)

characterizes him as "the hero, the embodiment of the unified medieval soul. He comes as the superman and as the demigod; his morality is spiritualized and exploded by the perfect combination of classical virtue."[167]

With a division between good and evil as such, the categorizations Morris creates seem somewhat at odds. Why should one suppose Gardner means for us to see Hrothgar as more dishonorable than Unferth? Giving both characters in the novel the best possible spin (assuming Morris sees Gardner as expecting us to disregard Grendel's view of them as equally self-serving and ridiculous), neither seems more willing to sacrifice his life for the kingdom. In the novel, both are seen as willing to do battle to sacrifice their lives for what they call glory. There is also the matter of the *Beowulf* poet's approbation of Hrothgar and its general disdain for Unferth, though neither of them is able to protect the kingdom from Grendel or his mother.

Butts distinguishes the Beowulf character from the dragon, noting that angels also have wings, Beowulf's wings are described as blindingly white, and just prior to Beowulf's arrival Grendel has noticed the impressions of snow angels left by children, furthering the association.[168] Other scholars as well have found renewal as the theme here, with Beowulf's actions secondary (or perhaps necessary) for such a renewal. Ronald Nutter characterizes it this way, "In the final chapter of the novel, representing the twelfth sign of the zodiac, Pisces, or the Fish, Grendel and Beowulf finally confront one another . . . Grendel knows now that his life is coming to an end, and that the man killing him represents a new age, inspired to art by noble acts. This art will be like fish, on which people might be nourished until the spring of their rebirth."[169]

Referencing Beowulf and the song that he makes Grendel sing about destruction and renewal, "The wall will fall to the wind as the windy hill will fall, and all things thought in former times; Nothing made remains, nor man remembers. And these towns shall be called the shining towns," and then Beowulf's comment after this, "The world will burn green. Sperm build again," Helen B. Ellis and Warren U. Ober comment on the victor's philosophy as he kills Grendel, "Beowulf's promise to Grendel is

[167] (Morris, *A World of Order and Light*, 54-55)
[168] (Butts, *The Novels of John Gardner*, 89)
[169] (Nutter, *A Dream of Peace*, 74)

the promise of Gardner's work itself, that . . . there is—and always will be— renewal."[170]

David Cowart has noted that despite an apocalyptic framework (as he perceives it) in the poem, no mention is ever made of Armageddon. This, Cowart believes, comes from the poet's stubborn refusal to acknowledge the New Testament in any way, perhaps hoping instead that his audience would more readily identify Beowulf with Christ: "God in his wisdom can allow a shrewd and valiant hero to overcome the enemy of rational order, Grendel . . . But the pre-revelation god of Hrothgar and Hygelac cannot overcome mutability itself, the destructive matter inherent in matter, slave to Fate—the principle traditionally represented in the figure of the dragon. The world of Beowulf is doomed. Men die, nations die, eventually the world itself will die."[171] (79-80)

Cowart's ideas correspond well to Gardner's explanation of Beowulf's dragon-like aspects. In an interview with Paul Ferguson, Gardner addressed issues that readers had been having about the novel's representation of the poem's hero. When Ferguson asks about Beowulf seeming to become the dragon, Gardner replies, "There's Christ the Dragon and there's Satan the Dragon. There's always a war between these two great dragons. In modern Christian symbolism a sweeter image of Jesus with the sheep in his arms has evolved, but I like the old image of the warring dragon."[172] The image of Christ as a "warring dragon," as opposed to the loving shepherd, corresponds to Christ in Revelation, which would explain the dragon imagery corresponding to Beowulf's heartlessness and cruelty to Grendel in the novel.

Of the last battle in *Beowulf*, Gardner says this, "And the dragon episode may have to do, on its deepest level, with Armageddon and Last Judgment . . . The irony is dramatic: the Christ toward whom Beowulf's life and character point (like a "beacon") redeems what would have seemed, before revelation, the tragedy of Beowulf the good man."[173] The question is whether one then sees the *Beowulf* poet dismissing notions of

---

[170] Helen B. Ellis and Warren U. Ober, "Grendel and Blake: The Contraries of Existence" (*John Gardner, Critical Perspectives*. Eds. Robert A. Morace and Kathryn VanSpanckeren, Carbondale: Southern Illinois UP), 56

[171] (Cowart, *Arches & Light*, 79-80)

[172] (Ferguson, "John Gardner: The Art of Fiction LXXIII," 146) Howell refers to the interview (in its published, prose form) and sees Gardner's explanation thus, "The association of dragon imagery with Christ has less currency for most readers, and Gardner acknowledged the problem of interpretation when he explained that he had in mind the two dragons of medieval art," *Understanding John Gardner*, 82)

[173] (Gardner, *The Construction of Christian Poetry in Old English*, 84)

salvation as found in the New Testament (as Cowart seems to suggest) or, in fact, promoting it. Many others have noted Christ-like motifs in *Beowulf*, with the suggestion of the Anglo-Saxon hero's role as a member of human society being similar to Christ's salvation of mankind. Specifically, Whallon discusses the poem's apparently purposeful correlations between Beowulf and Christ, including symbolic numeric details such as the twelve men who accompany Beowulf to the dragon's lair, with the thirteenth as "Judas" stealing the cup that incites the beast's rage and, in effect, causes Beowulf's death—a cup worth "thirty pieces of silver." Also, he notes that the "three synoptic Gospels agree that a darkness lasted over the land for three hours, from the sixth to the ninth hour" and that Beowulf's comrades wait for him three hours, thinking him dead while he battles Grendel's mother; he returns to the surface with Grendel's head at the ninth hour.[174]

Gardner himself posits that while Beowulf may prefigure Christ on the historical and "tropological" levels, he may "directly represent him" on the anagogical level follows the continuation of this idea in some detail: "In overcoming an enemy from the underworld for all the people, through his own power, Beowulf is analogous to Christ: he does for the Danes, within the physical domain of flesh and blood monsters, what Christ does in the spiritual domain when he overcomes the devil for all mankind."[175] Note that for Gardner such an allegorical connection is fraught with contradictions, "Clearly, the relationship between Christ and Beowulf can be seen as, at least on one level, ironic" (84).

Green shows links between the dragon and his treasure in "The Book of Revelation," further equating the fires of the poem, particularly the funeral of Beowulf, with imagery "reminiscent of the fire of doomsday." Speaking of the dragon in *Beowulf*, Green states: "On one level of association, the dragon's destruction of the Geats' hall and his killing of their king open the way to the ultimate collapse of the Geats as a nation. The destruction of the microcosmic center of the Geats associates the dragon with apocalyptic events. Standing at the center of Part Two, and presiding over the ultimate destruction of man's world, the dragon of *Beowulf* has reminded more than one reader of the dragon of the apocalypse . . . "[176]

As in the poem and Beowulf's fatal third battle with the dragon, Grendel's death in his third battle is attended by his fierce loyalty to a

---

[174] (Whallon, "The Christianity of *Beowulf*," 83-84)

[175] (Gardner, *The Construction of Christian Poetry in Old English*, 61)

[176] (Green, "Man, Time, and Apocalypse in *The Wanderer, The Seafarer, and Beowulf*," 293-295)

creed. While Beowulf displays unwavering trust in the Almighty, it would seem that Grendel asserts his nihilism by proclaiming the mortal wound inflicted on him by Beowulf to be the result of "Accident!" The status of both protagonists initiates their participation in a final fight and ends their earthly existence in a way confirming their creed. As a function of primus and an attempt to maintain his status, Gardner's Grendel fights his own dragon at the end of the novel and loses his life. As he stands at the edge of the chasm, mortally wounded, he is surrounded by a group of animals who have gathered to watch him die, just as Beowulf's death is attended by those who could not match his prowess on earth.

Salvation for Grendel himself, considered separately from the world, may be found in his final statement, if one sees it as an extension outward from the animals watching him, to humankind and, perhaps, the reader in particular: "Poor Grendel's had an accident—so may you all" (174). In *On Becoming a Novelist*, Gardner stated that Grendel's final proclamation was in fact a moment of moral alliance with a higher power, "So for all his conscious belief that it's all accident, Grendel chooses death, morally aligning himself with God."[177]

Perhaps a further understanding of what he means by this may be drawn from Gardner's comment concerning the end of *Beowulf*: "The central irony of the poem, and the basis of its ironic conclusion, is that prior to the revelation of God's plan, the heroic ethic by which God works does not visibly operate on earth, where it seems no man is finally paid as he deserves because all men die. The best one can hope for is lasting 'dom,' a word which means one thing to the pagan, another thing—more joyful—to the Christian."[178]

Clearly, Grendel is not a Christian, so the final words of the novel may mean his acceptance of his doom rather than a negation of it. Gardner's reflection on the novel's ending as showing Grendel's alliance with God in these final moments may signal to us that Grendel's atheism (wherein all events in life and nature have been for Grendel 'mindless,' without a divine plan) has shifted. Since Beowulf has mortally wounded him in combat, he cannot be seen as choosing death over life at the moment when he stands on the cliff's edge, yet Chapters Ten through Twelve signal death's approach in no uncertain terms. His joy at the end of his tedium causes him to disregard all of the signs: he goes to the mead hall to encounter Beowulf anyway, either ignoring or accepting the fact that he will die from doing so. In the poem, Beowulf as an aged king, enters his

[177] John Gardner, *On Becoming a Novelist* (New York: Harper and Row), 59

[178] (Gardner, *The Construction of Christian Poetry in Old English*, 64)

battle with the dragon knowing that it may be his last, yet choosing the creed for which his life stood.

In terms of allegory about the fall of man, the third battle in the novel certainly ends with Grendel's doom, and if Grendel in the novel represents modern (unredeemed) man through his connection to Cain, then the penultimate fight with Beowulf indeed equates to Beowulf's death at the hands of the dragon. In both cases, the deeper question involves redemption and salvation, on the spiritual level. On the practical level, one may see that Grendel, no matter what he considers the cause of his death, reaches outward to a wider audience and sees beyond himself, one of the few such occasions of this in the novel.

If Grendel is addressing such an audience, even the reader, the next question becomes whether he's conferring a curse or a blessing on them. If this is a curse, one could see him as coming to his maximum level of monstrosity, in conferring a horrendous, painful, purposeless death outward to unseen perceivers. If it is a blessing, if Grendel wishes his audience to have the accident that will finally and fully connect them to their doom (be it for good or ill), then this final moment is a conversion for him, one that he projects outward. In any case, it is still an act of communication and bonding.

Grendel and Gardner's Theories on Fiction Writing

John Gardner's recasting of *Beowulf* in the form of a modern novel with a first-person protagonist opens with Grendel near the end of his twelve-year reign of terror, a character both familiar and unfamiliar to readers of the poem. Familiarity comes from the situation, its conflict and its bloodshed. Grendel has been attacking the mead hall with merciless intent for more than a decade, nearly destroying the community of Hrothgar and his once-proud Danes. While Gardner presents us with a creature driven by rage to sadistic aggression, the voice of Grendel himself is surprisingly intelligent, sensitive, and artistic, as well as self-reflective.

Scholars interpret this in various ways. This complexity, both ironic in its seeming distance from the *Beowulf* monster and at the same time somewhat modern in its explication of mental processes, reinforces the focus on Grendel's personality and the evolution of his identity. Nutter calls Grendel the "truth teller of the story . . . for those critics who believe Grendel to be a nihilistic black-humor satire of contemporary life," and he adds, "For those familiar with Gardner's work, Grendel, though in some ways worthy of our sympathy, is, nonetheless, a monster, a destroyer of human accomplishments and a mocker of human endeavors."[179] In *Understanding John Gardner*, John Howell comes closest to locating Grendel within the bounds of a traditional protagonist. For Howell, Grendel is a sympathetic character, even " . . . a potentially warm-hearted creature who is so hurt by the rejection of human beings that he ends up eating them," and he notes the comparison to Dr. Frankenstein's creature, and adds, " . . . who also inspired a poem and a libretto by Gardner."[180]

Gardner's intentions for *Grendel's* overall form and themes have produced a good deal of scholarly speculation. To some extent, matters are complicated by apparent discrepancies in Gardner's stated positions, in interviews and elsewhere. In such interviews, Gardner's dynamic charisma reveals itself as a rapid-fire exchange of ideas combined with surprising interjections. While fascinating, this style lends itself to overstatement and, at times, contradiction.

Perhaps the most puzzling of these dialogues is Gardner's first substantial interview after the publication of *Grendel*, with Digby Diehl. In it, he makes a number of statements rebelling against the accepted ideals in the poem, "I teach *Beowulf* all of the time and think that it is the most undersold poem in the language. But I don't really like the value system, the concept of heroism. Really, the hero is a guy who kills a lot of people and grabs a lot of gold. These are Bad Guys." As is typical of some of his interviews, he continues somewhat blithely, "Grendel the monster is a sort of a Sartrean anarchist who kills himself over a momentary failure of ideals. Sartre is sick and evil, psychotic in fact, as Camus pointed out."[181]

For a very different view, consider this statement from Gardner in *The Construction of Christian Poetry in Old English*, "*Beowulf* is clearly a work in which the pagan intuition of Hrothgar and Beowulf anticipates revelation. It is just as clearly, on one level, a celebration of the best possible human—perhaps divinely inspired—code. Christianity wins by default on this level, and the points at which the life of Beowulf calls to mind the life of Christ can be understood as signals of the level's central irony. If in terms of the ethic of noble service, wisdom, and reward, Beowulf seems cheated in his old age (his joy as he dies is partly delusion), so all good men must appear to be cheated prior to man's knowledge of Christ, who can raise the dead and pay them as they deserve."[182]

---

[179] (Nutter, *A Dream of Peace*, 74)

[180] (Howell, *Understanding John Gardner*, 63)

[181] Digby Diehl, "Medievalist in Illinois Ozarks" (*Conversations with John Gardner*), 3-4

[182] (Gardner, *The Construction of Christian Poetry in Old English*, 83)

Further, in the Diehl interview, comparing his fiction to those of his contemporaries, Gardner likens himself to postmodernists past and present: "I have nothing to say except that I think words are beautiful. I'm a stylist; for me, everything is rhythm and rhyme. There are a handful of other stylists like Gass, Elkin, Barthelme, Barth and Ralph Ellison who have nothing to say either. We just write. I guess Samuel Beckett is the model for all of us, which is ironic since he descends from Joyce, who still thought he could save the world with literature."[183] The attitude Gardner takes with Diehl toward the purposes and function of his own art seems wildly out of sync with his later proclamations in *On Moral Fiction*, *On Becoming a Novelist*, and *The Art of Fiction*, as well as countless interviews and articles: indeed, nearly everywhere else, after 1972. It is, as well, out of character with the great respect he affords medieval literature, both before the Diehl interview (such as his 1965 critical introduction to *The Complete Works of the Gawain Poet*).

The questions raised by such an interview, particularly as they apply to Grendel, the release of which prompted the interview, are many. Most especially, did Gardner consider it a postmodern piece with "nothing to say"? While one is tempted to take this interview at face value, the next substantive interview with Gardner concerning Grendel came a year later. Howell paraphrases Gardner's statements thus, "Grendel also experiences a profound sense of alienation but is ultimately forced to feel and as a consequence dies knowing he is connected to the world."[184] If the novel reflects such a paradigm (and I think it does), this would be an amazing feat for an author who truly had "nothing to say."

At this time, the nature of Gardner's classification of himself amidst his peers begins to change. An increasingly critical tone emerges, particularly regarding postmodernist writing—again, very different from the Diehl interview. By the end of 1973, Gardner in his speeches and interviews begins calling for a rejection of nihilism. By the time of the Bellamy interview, Gardner still allies himself with Gass and Barthelme, but sees himself as distinct in terms of his ethical approaches to fiction, a vastly different persona than one who would see himself as literary descendent of Beckett with an "ironic" connection to Joyce. By this point, his analysis of *Grendel*, both the novel's form and the title character, has changed, as has his definition of himself as a postmodernist.

With the publication of *On Moral Fiction* in 1978, Gardner has much to say and says it with unabashed bluntness, much to the chagrin of the

---

[183] (Diehl, "Medievalist in Illinois Ozarks," 4)

[184] John Howell, *John Gardner: A Bibliographic Profile* (Carbondale: Southern Illinois UP), 86

literary community and some of his critical and scholarly supporters. In the book, he criticizes Gass, Barth, and Barthelme, among others, and seems to take on postmodernism in general, not to mention many modern fiction writers. The book made him a literary celebrity and, as such, also made him a target for those who disagreed with his assessments. As for *Grendel*, he does not retroactively apply this shift in attitude; if indeed he wrote the novel with nothing to say and as a stylist, he seems in retrospect to have found new meaning in the novel.

An answer to this seeming contradiction may be seen in the separation Gardner sees between the process of writing and the product itself. Gardner's central tenets on art embody this idea: while art should aim for truth, the artistic process is one which champions the imagination, not reason, as the wellspring of such truth. In *On Moral Fiction*, as in other works, he claims art that has a connection to truth which seems symbiotic and without conscious structure, "Art is as original and important as it is precisely because it does not start out with a clear knowledge of what it means to say. Out of the artist's imagination, as out of nature's inexhaustible well, pours one thing after another. The artist composes, writes, or paints just as he dreams, seizing whatever swims close to his net." Indeed, he asserts the necessity of unbridled invention to morality, "Art, in sworn opposition to chaos, discovers by its process what it can say. That is art's morality."[185]

This idea of the creative experience as dream state runs throughout Gardner's proposals, crossing the boundaries between his modes, and seems to presuppose a cogent simpatico between the conscious and unconscious intentions of an artist. Some have suggested even more. Cowart notes, "Gardner thus modifies the traditional dictum that art uncovers changeless, preexistent truths; he makes the proposition 'life imitates art' something more than a parlor witticism."[186] In any case, Gardner's theories allow for the artist to create art without any conscious determination of meaning, yet for this process to create a work containing meaning nonetheless.

As for *Grendel*, the question of its meaning remains. Specifically, how do dark humor and ironic inversions affect it? Of the poem's relationship to the novel, Klinkowitz says, "Myths need to be retold, because from generation to generation we forget them . . . But what happens to a myth's morality when its structure is diametrically reversed . . . Does the myth

---

[185] (Gardner, *On Moral Fiction*, 13-14)
[186] (Cowart, *Arches & Light*, 10)

itself take on inverted value . . . ?"[187] Klinkowitz does not answer the question, but it is central to unraveling the paradoxes of the novel. If Grendel-as-monster sees human values such as heroism and community traditions as ridiculous, does this necessarily imply the mocking of such values in traditional art such as *Beowulf*?

In such a case, the meaning of the inverted work would seem a repudiation of values, or at least the depiction of them by artists, which, one has to admit, functions well within Gardner's claim in the Diehl interview of Beowulf being a "Bad Guy" who "who kills a lot of people and grabs a lot of gold." Grendel, as non-human is, after all, removed from the social need for values. In this paradigm, the novel parodies the darkness of life through an ironic perspective. As readers, one assumes, we are meant to take the joke as a critique of Anglo-Saxon values and a critique of modern ideas such as existentialism, which Gardner in the same interview connects to *Grendel*. But if this is all he means to be doing in the novel, then its meaning is quite dark indeed, summed up this way: human endeavors toward greatness and the gathering of wealth in Anglo-Saxon times were ridiculous (as were the heroes who protected those values) and modern man's attempt to see himself as separate from others is ridiculous as well—in short, as a species we have worked ourselves into a paradox of values.

One objection to such a pessimistic view on Gardner's theories is the contradictory stance it would seem to take with Gardner's other novels and his treatises like *On Moral Fiction*. A closer look at that work shows this is not the case. Yet even if one allowed it, the "anomaly work of art" may be found within the realm of any artist's scope: there need be no law of consistency among an artist's works, especially if experimentation is at the heart of creativity. Some scholars see *Grendel* as a moment in Gardner's creative works of darkly humorous detachment about the human condition and mankind's more pitiful attempts at constructing ideals, after which he moved on to works containing more by way of life affirmation.

Such a view would seem to tie up the loose ends, but a further quandary, for me, comes from a sense of *Grendel* as being more important than this, not just as it may fit within Gardner's other works, but as a work in and of itself. While darkly humorous, *Grendel* nonetheless signifies serious inquiry about life on a variety of levels. The characterization of Grendel as a viable protagonist who struggles for an understanding of moral values, as well as Gardner's own respect for and scholarly contribution

[187] Jerome Klinkowitz, "John Gardner's *Grendel*" (*John Gardner, Critical Perspectives*, eds. Morace and VanSpankeren), 64

to medieval studies in literature, not to mention the paralleling and allegorical nods to the poem, all point to a more genuine intention than is generally afforded the novel by those who see it as a kind of joke.

What seems most clear from the text is Gardner's conscious attempt to promote Grendel as a sympathetic character, not merely to enhance the irony and the humor (though it does this) but indeed to urge readers toward Grendel's new perspective on mankind (and ourselves) differing from the famous poem's narrative. Such approaches are plentiful in commercial and literary works, from Mary Shelley's *Frankenstein* to Gregory Maguire's 1995 novel *Wicked*, the *Wizard of Oz* from the Wicked Witch of the West's viewpoint.

The differences in the examples bear note, for while Shelley's intention is for readers to take the creature seriously, to invest in him as a protagonist worth caring about, Maguire means for his readers to enjoy the satire of an inverted children's tale. In my opinion, Grendel sometimes seems a restless alliance of these two approaches; the serious focus on character development and voice within an unrealistic milieu is reminiscent of *Frankenstein*, yet the ironic reversal of a familiar story and the playful burlesque and lampooning of both *Beowulf* and modern philosophy leans toward darkly humorous satire.

Admittedly, the latter tendency makes it harder for one to accept Gardner as trumpeting the monster's view of reality as both accurate and moral (and in this way, life affirming). The same is true when it comes to discussing the novel as meaningful art, even if its meaning comes as a byproduct of the artistic process and not as conscious design. In my experience, most readers feel led by Gardner to care for Grendel and see him as viable protagonist, as one struggling against the hardships of his circumstances, and not simply as a prose component of dark humor or an exercise in linguistic beauty. To see *Grendel* as only a vehicle of humor is to ignore the ethical foundations of the monster's observations, as well as to set aside an awareness of the seriousness with which Gardner approached literature.

Nor would it seem especially easy to create a sympathetic narrator from the monster, particularly if one posits the creature's brutality and bloodlust, as does Gardner from the outset. Yet despite the evil of Grendel's actions, Gardner's focus on the evolution of identity from innocence to depravity makes the monster's decisions logical as a response to his environment, not only the setting of his living conditions, but his isolation from his own kin as well as the animals, the cosmic climate of his environment, and the humans denying him fellowship because of his supposed evil ancestry. What's worse is that the denial comes in the form of poetry so beautiful that Grendel himself is moved to agree with the Shaper.

The irony, as I see it, comes from Grendel's non-human status: if he were simply to accept his monstrous identity as outcast from society, he could live as happily and simply as lions, sharks, or any other carnivore. His desire to be part of a human tribe, even as he is excluded from it, leads to his rage and anguish. His story is not merely one of ironic inversion, with humor resulting from the "monster as hero": Grendel's is a story about an outsider's need for community in all its forms, social, sexual, religious, and artistic, and most especially about the transmutation of ego when this is denied him. (As for *Beowulf*, while one would not call this the poem's central concern, the human characteristics of Grendel and his mother suggest the presence of the same idea, even a thousand years ago.)

The intention on Gardner's part to make Grendel a character whose personality evolves, and not merely an ironic figure of dark humor, may be seen as well in the structure of the novel. While beginning with Grendel at nearly the end of his twelve-year war with Hrothgar, and the human hero vanquisher about to appear in the story, the chapters which follow become a protracted digression, with Chapter Two opening as an explanation of Grendel's childhood and early adolescence; the plot returns to the poem's presentation of Grendel only in the last two chapters. Howell sees the flashback as ending in Chapter Eight, when Grendel returns to the present moment of his telling. This accurately describes the narrative flow, for Chapters Nine and Ten "anticipate Beowulf's arrival, and foreshadow Grendel's death."[188]

However, since the poem focuses on Beowulf rather than Grendel, the chapters foreshadowing their battle seem to function more as part of the cause-and-effect narrative, less as a reflection of the current action. While the novel does narrate events from the poem, most of the action comes in flashbacks serving as precursors and explanations (from Grendel's perspective) of his becoming the self-proclaimed "Grendel, Ruiner of Meadhalls, Wrecker of Kings!" (80). Gardner presents us with a biographical novel, Grendel at its core, irony and humor coming from our previous understanding of the poem's central action.

In providing *Grendel* with structural elements corresponding to the poem's, Gardner creates an allegory encoded with a variety of signifiers, including Judeo-Christian ones, modern philosophical views expressed by Sartre, Nietzsche, Whitehead, and others. Some may suggest that the very juxtaposition of existentialism onto a medieval paradigm engenders

---

[188] (Howell, *Understanding John Gardner*, 63)

parody. Yet this may also be seen as parallel to the *Beowulf* poet's use of pagan material. Writing in a period after existentialism, he is free to draw on its ideas for his themes, themes which will resound more with his post-existentialist audience; thus, like the medieval writers whom he admires, Gardner takes authorial license and uses whatever he finds convenient for his purposes.

For Gardner to do so within *Grendel*, while transforming the material and characters of the original poem, does not necessarily challenge its vision—as it would more likely do if it were a postmodern, purely satiric, or absurdist piece. While the definitions do not necessarily exclude one another, "recasting" implies Gardner's expanse of the original elements to create a new work with an encoded system of values and meanings—one that will resonate for a modern audience as a whole system, and not merely exist in ironic contrast to the prototype.

The difference is not limited to whether one sees the novel as standing on its own merits, but in how one assesses Gardner's view of the poem and his use of it, particularly as this relates to a moral scheme for the novel. To be sure, Gardner means for his readers to find humor in the recast of events and characters, but does the use of humor mean he sees the poem as having a flawed vision? Further, is the humor that comes from inverting one of the greatest heroic poems all Gardner hopes to provide, or even the major point of what he provides?

If this were so, why does he dedicate himself to such a detailed explication of the poem's structure when those things in and of themselves do not add to the humor? Nor do they, in and of themselves, suggest parody: Grendel's attack on Wealtheow is no less horrible or "more humorous" than Beowulf's fight with Grendel's mother. If the inversion is not for the purposes of ironic humor, then perhaps he means to be constructing a similar allegorical paradigm. The suggestion is worthy of pursuit, not only in its basic logic, but in its answer to questions raised by the novel.

To do so raises the level of inquiry into the sorts of truths and conclusions readers may draw from the novel's vision, from the most basic of good versus evil, or redemption versus destruction, to Grendel's perspective as an outcast. If the novel is meant to be more than an experiment in irony, what deeper implications might be spun from Grendel's struggle to define himself? Indeed, how may such questions correlate to similar questions found in the poem? The deeper query moves from "Why does Grendel struggle so hard to define himself, most especially if he alone exists?" since the answer to this seems limited to a polemic against the illogic of existentialism (and is therefore somewhat small in scope), to "How does the struggle for individual identity define and underscore humankind's unique place in nature?" and more, "How does such a struggle vary when one shifts factors in the environment, including physical, spiritual, and philosophical aspects, and how does it remain universal?" The answers to this certainly point to Gardner's views on the failure of existentialism, but they do much more as well.

One of the central tenets of *Beowulf* is the need for balance between individual desire and the needs of the community, while at the same time paying strict attention to the dictates of God and allowing for the whims of fate, wyrd, and doom. This is also one of the central tenets of the novel, in Grendel's displacement from the community and his ironic situation notwithstanding. While one may dispute the relativity of modern ideas concerning free will and determinism to their Anglo-Saxon counterparts, the larger questions remain: to what extent are an individual's actions under the auspices of a controlling universal force, to what extent are they a reflection of some other plan (such as nature) in which God may or may not participate, and to what extent are they a mirror of a creature's need or will?

As I see it, Gardner spins out the possibilities of these many questions within the context of Grendel's search for his identity. Grendel is more than just an experiment in disputing modern theories and satirizing medieval ones; as I see it, where John Gardner disputes ideas, in modern modes, he is doing precisely as did the *Beowulf* poet in Anglo-Saxon modes. Cowart points out these similarities of thematic examination: " . . . the author of *Grendel* surveys, in the various ideas taken up, the possibilities for optimism about the human condition, and in this respect the novel does not differ radically from the Ur-story, *Beowulf*. Projecting a fatalistic awareness of man's mortality and the mutability of all his glories, the *Beowulf*-poet also 'surveys' the claims of statecraft, familial love, heroism, and loyalty to gainsay the passing of all things: great men, great beauty, great nations. *Beowulf* at once endorses and questions the values of the society it describes . . . "[189]

Some of the themes inherent in Grendel's perspective correspond faithfully to those of the poem: both works recognize a conflict in the need to establish individuality and gain personal power while maintaining a connection and a submissive posture to a higher force—be it God, nature, the Dragon, one's prince, one's heritage, the power of art, oneself or the community at large. While Cowart may be right in man's need to "banish . . . his own baser instincts" (41) by attempting to keep Grendel out of the

[189] (Cowart, *Arches & Light*, 44)

mead hall, a closer look at the instincts themselves seems to be called for. Clearly, in the poem, the domination of an individual over a group is not considered, in and of itself, to be a base desire.

Domination of others, if the cause is right, seems integral to Anglo-Saxon society. Moreover, it defines Scyld, as a character in his own right, and as a "good king." The rightness of the cause depends of course on one's own situation as well as the (sometimes unclear) will of God; the effects of Fate ("dom") play into the conflict. Thus, one of the original precepts of the poem, domination is a way of life, seems strange, perhaps, to a modern society of democratic principles. We would like to think ourselves better than this, our ways more inclusive, our strategies less related to our actual strength of arms. If Grendel's first appearance in *Beowulf*, storming the mead-hall and terrifying the inhabitants, had he been recognizable as a "human" invader with a "human" force behind him, would have led to his having been hailed a good king by his people.

Is Grendel's dominance in the poem evil because of his outcast state (not for the mere fact of its dominance)? If so, and if Gardner's novel explains the relation to Cain *as not Grendel's fault* (for how could it be?), then is the dominance itself warranted as an expression of individuality, a search for identity? Gardner scholars including Morris, Nutter, and Butts seem to categorize Gardner's idea in the novel as Grendel is evil, either an evil expression of the dark side of our human natures, or the representation of the immoral artist, or the symbolic epitome of destructive forces. Others, such as Howell, maintain Grendel's violence as an ironic counterpoint to the poem's vision of heroism.

Another perspective may be gained from assessing Grendel as a creature of nature whose evil tendencies result from his interaction with humans, much as Frankenstein's monster reacts first in innocence, and then with learned cunning. The question of identity becomes paramount. As a close textual analysis shows, the novel opens with a chapter where nearly every passage concerns Grendel attempting to define himself in relation to his environment in order to dominate it, or the reverse of this, to dominate his environment in order to define himself. The irony here is in the fact of his being like Cain, an outcast, and so having no community or higher power for whom to give this tribute, or from whom to receive codes of behavior. His assertion of individuality, therefore, has no social relevance and therefore no importance in the (human) world.

On a larger scale, the irony of the situation is humorous—the monster has no one to talk to because he kills people, but he kills people out of anger due to his loneliness; he talks to himself and by extension via the vehicle of the novel, to John Gardner's readers, incidentally "also people."

On a smaller scale, the conflict concerns the necessary bond between individual identity and audience. In terms of the interior narrative, Grendel's audience consists principally of a human community horrified by his exploits—and so it becomes worthwhile to note his numerous and desperate attempts at constructing other audience platforms: natural, supernatural, familial, and individual (by addressing himself.)

As illustrated by a close survey of the text, identity becomes central to Grendel's creation of himself. Ultimately, his failure to find stability or happiness comes from his inability to see himself objectively, either as a distinctly separate individual—one without a need for outside reference points—or as a creature functioning within a cosmological scheme. While some may say such a paradigm reflects the condition of "modern man," it seems to me to reflect the universal human condition. Certainly, the *Beowulf* poet in the opening defines Scyld relative to his society, linking his goodness to his role as provider for his people, showing the direct connection between his assertion of individuality—his personal identity—and his role as leader and provider. While the poet certainly could discuss the battles which Scyld led and the thanes whom he inspired to fight with him, the focus is on Scyld as an individual dominator.

One of the central questions becomes whether one sees Gardner's protagonist as responsible for his situation. Are we meant to take his destruction of others as a humorous parody of domination gone wrong—that is, not "the good king" but "the good monster"? His relative greatness is reflected in his ability to "take" and to "terrify." Further, questions of lineage and their relation to identity surface in the novel and the poem. Scyld arrives as an orphan of mysterious origin, and makes his own reputation. The poet, as he goes on to discuss Scyld's line of descendants, explains the connection between God and life on earth, "Afterwards a son was born to him . . . whom God sent to comfort the people: He had seen the sore need they had suffered . . . Therefore, the Lord of Life, the Ruler of Heaven, gave him honor in the world . . . "[190]

For Grendel in the poem, however, lineage and any relationship to God comes in the form of negative bonds, and his description as an outcast connects him to those doomed by the Almighty, "Unhappy creature, he lived for a time in the home of the monsters' race, after God had condemned them as kin of Cain. The Eternal Lord avenged the murder in which he slew Abel." In the passage, Grendel's unhappiness is linked to his living situation and his outcast state, previously designated by God to the kin of Cain. Just prior to the lines above quoted, Grendel's attack of

---

[190] (Donaldson, *trans*., *Beowulf*, 5)

the mead hall is explained by his "painfully endured hardship . . . for every day he heard loud mirth in the hall."[191]

The monster's conscious awareness of God is not clear, nor is God's specific condemnation of Grendel the individual. However, the connection between the attacks and the loneliness gives Grendel human emotion and explains his actions within a human context: thus, while indeed he is a "creature of evil," "savage and cruel," he is as well a feeling being forced to live as an outcast and reacting to the situation with human emotion. If one sees Grendel as pure wickedness and sees the novel's allegories as incidental only, based on the derived nature of the work, then the first-person outlook is without moral value (except as a possible lesson in amorality) and the novel becomes a reversed fable about good and evil, what some would call postmodern in its ironic inversions.

In the end, the evil monster is killed by the good hero, order is restored, and the irony comes from Gardner having created a likeable 'evil protagonist.' Some of the most respected Gardner scholars propose that if a moral scheme is to come from the novel's approach, then it must be in the inverse, with at least one of the humans as a paradigm of moral virtue. To this way of thinking, "life affirmation" as described in Gardner's *On Moral Fiction* comes in their survival, through art, culture, patience, or strength, and the monster's demise. The suggestion would be that readers will know better than to side with the ferocious beast, and will see the irony or understand joke.

Likewise, Gregory L. Morris sees Gardner using ideas of the tripartite soul in the novel in an ironic way, with some humans representative of distorted values while others reflect the positive (54-58). Others see Grendel's view of society as twisted by his own insanity. Per Winther sees Grendel as "schizophrenic" (166) and one whose "absolutist inclinations get in the way of a fair assessment of human values" (168); otherwise, he suggests, the monster would see the humans more realistically, with both positive and negative attributes. Gardner, such a study suggests, wants us to understand that humans are not nearly as bad as Grendel paints them; he wants us to see Grendel's madness as the lesson.

In my view, such assessments shift the burden of Grendel's alienated perspective to his inner failures. Yes, Grendel becomes more and more locked within his mental world, but isn't this a direct result of being locked out of society? Can he be blamed for locking himself out? In every chapter, he tries to become closer to humans, and even in his monstrosity he finds a way to fit into their definitions. Is this a reflection of freakish

---

[191] (Donaldson, *trans*., *Beowulf*, 3-5)

madness, simple-minded Grendel who is swayed by the Dragon, either inside himself or outside? What changes Grendel (and he is not blameless in this change), is the influence of humankind. It seems to me more likely that Gardner is criticizing our penchant for projecting our failings onto the most convenient targets. In Grendel's case, he looks alien and doesn't speak their language, so they assume he's condemned by their religion.

In a modern context, as I see it, the poem's morals apply on a straight parallel, not as a parody, and the novel then goes beneath the poem's proposals to investigate cause. One may assume a certain universality, and can assume the Anglo-Saxons, too, found themselves focused on the self at the expense of the greater community; this certainly seems to be true as one of the many tenets of the poem. In Gardner's novel, the focus on self widens to include egocentricity on the social level as well, excluding those like Grendel who are different.

By making such individuals into pariahs and refusing entry, society creates its own shocking monsters—creates them in its own image, though the image becomes twisted by projections of transgression so that the abject locates itself in repulsion and becomes outcast further. The novel need not be a happy one to be life affirming. Many tragedies affirm life, as Gardner maintains. The question is whether a lesson may be learned or whether, as in some postmodern works, the tragedy is portrayed merely because such things happen. Extending this, one may ask what lesson may be learned from *Grendel*.

Grendel in the novel fails because he cannot see himself objectively, as a creature functioning within a cosmological scheme. This is why Adam and Eve fail, and why Cain fails (and also Gilgamesh, Icarus, or name your mythos and you'll find a dozen): the immediate concern with self-gain overrides the rules established in a larger design by culture. From the start, Grendel sees the world as without a creator: "The sun spins mindlessly . . . as if by plan" (7) repeated (138) "The sky says nothing, predictably" (6) and "The cold night air is reality at last: indifferent to me as a stone face carved on a high wall to show that the world is abandoned" (9). If one is going to blame him for such a position, it seems to me, we must first address the issue of his having been told that such a Creator would not allow creatures such as Grendel to be part of the kingdom.

The humans have taught him this (not his mother, not the Dragon), each of whom is preoccupied with their own goals. Grendel wants to believe in a god, any god, so that eventually he makes himself into a god. Amazingly, the humans then accept him as a kind of "supra" natural force, not just Ork who mistakes him for the Great Destroyer and worships him, but the Shaper as well whom, we assume in his singing a "heavier harp song now," in fact begins telling the tale of the attacks by the hell-creature in verse.

Grendel has no objectivity, no way to see himself from an outside perspective. As a direct result of human rejection, he is drawn toward definitions which allow him to exist, even if it means he is in complete isolation; "I alone exist" (22), he thinks, before his mother comes to rescue him. Surely this is so, but the only way to combat it or to reverse it is to intercede in some positive way, which no one in the novel does—even Unferth, caught too completely in his own self-centered universe to speak with the monster in a meaningful way—similarly Ork has a chance to converse with Grendel but cannot see him as anything other than the Great Destroyer.

Grendel knows his creation of the world through thought and language is not the actual world, "Talking, talking. Spinning a web of words, pale walls of dreams, between myself and all I see" (8), repeated throughout the story. This draws him toward the Shaper's art, which he sees as powerful, though not truthful. According to Grendel, the Shaper changed the world, but however powerful this Shaper's art may be, it is not truth, and so Grendel sees the hypocrisy of their religion and their art. He rejects a passive acceptance of this hypocrisy and instead he crafts an identity from it.

To deny this, or to suggest as does Per Winther that Gardner means for us to see such hypocrisy as the best possible attempts at survival in an uncertain and ill-defined world,[192] is to suggest Gardner's theme as one of compromise rather than the search for ultimate truth. It seems to me more likely that he means for us to understand his creature's anger at society, to identify with the anguish and the loneliness of being cast out. Grendel fails to realize that becoming the "brute existent" by which mankind defines itself will drive him further into madness.

Finally, I see no other analysis which explains in any convincing way the three major creative alterations of plot which Gardner makes boldly, even brazenly: first, Grendel's initial "attack" on the mead hall is a case of mistaken guilt where the humans charge him as a beast and murderer when in fact they themselves have perpetrated the crime; second, Grendel storms the mead hall and sexually assaults Wealtheow in a blatant and graphic way; third, when Beowulf begins to fight, he "becomes" a dragon in Grendel's mind. In the overall plot design, these three battles as they correlate between the two works is absolutely distinct. It gives us answers to questions which have lingered for too long.

---

[192] (Winther, *The Art of John Gardner*, 47A)

In addition, it provides new levels of analysis and a cogent system for interpreting symbols in all their forms, linear, vertical, and circular. Grendel as a modern "moral" allegory is neither the Old Testament salvation of the chosen people led into the Promised Land, nor the New Testament salvation of mankind by Christ. Grendel is Cain's kin—fully in the world at the start, outcast from God and separated from all things divine, a world like our own where existentialism and scientific rationalism have obscured notions of an omnipotent and ever-present Almighty. In Gardner's allegory, as I see it, Grendel as descendant of Cain is a kind of "double Adam," outcast for some original crime, similarly outcast for a connection to another crime, and shunned by society.

It is this second point which bears note: the failure or "fall" of society is in its projection of faults onto outsiders. The central conflict is not "good versus evil," but internal: the conflict of faith versus reason in a world in which the voice of God is silent, and the obligation of society—our society—to recognize our own faults, our tendency to project false definitions onto those whom we have outcast. They will, in the end, or some of them will, as Grendel does, adopt such monstrous definitions and attack us with unimaginable force. What society fails to realize is that they have, indeed, defined themselves by a monster created by their own warped projections. The horror of the abject becomes actualized into a highly destructive force.

Perhaps Grendel at the cliff redeems mankind by saving it from itself, from its own pride and arrogance. In effect, he may be saying to the reader, "Have the accident of discovering for yourself what you are." Perhaps the irony to which Gardner is pointing is not centered on the inversion of roles, but instead on the idea of humans creating the monster. In his novel, humans create the monster, inspire him to monstrosity, bolster his monstrous identity by defining him as such, and then consider themselves "saved" when they have destroyed him. Are we not those monsters, in so many ways? Gardner is not questioning the vision of the poem, but explaining it in modern terms. Grendel's continual desire to be part of the human community is itself an act of morality and heroism, given the obstacles before him. It is, as well, darkly ironic.

Some may say I have found nothing new in Gardner's *Grendel*, since of course the novel is derived, in more or less measure, from *Beowulf*. My goal has been to point to the poem as the foundation for the entire structure of the novel, not merely as a mimic of its core characters and events, but in the direct parallels between Beowulf's three battles and the three battles fought by Grendel. To do so is to see Gardner fashioning his ironic hero from the allegory and motifs of an Anglo-Saxon milieu, not in imitation or in parody, but as a tightly-woven recasting in its own right, with a moral scheme of life affirmation applicable most especially to our modern world, and with enough criticism of society to keep us busy for years, fixing it.

BIBLIOGRAPHY

Acker, Paul. 2006. "Horror and the Maternal in *Beowulf*." PMLA 121: 702-716.

Bellamy, Joe David and Pat Ensworth. 1973. "John Gardner." In *Conversations with John Gardner*, edited Allan Chavkin. University of Mississippi Press, 1990198.

Bonjour, Adrien. 1965. *Digressions in Beowulf.* Oxford: Basil Blackwell.

Butts, Leonard. 1988. *The Novels of John Gardner*. Baton Rouge: Louisiana State University Press.

Cain, Christopher M. 2006. Notes on "*Grendel* as Allegory." Submitted by Sandra Hiortdahl to *Introduction to Old English: English Department*, The Catholic University of America.

Carlson, Signe M. 1967. "The Monsters of *Beowulf*: Creations of Literary Scholars." *The Journal of American Folklore* 80.318, (Oct. 1967): 357-364.

Chambers, R.W. 1963. *Beowulf: An Introduction to the Study of the Poem*. Cambridge: Cambridge University Press.

Chance, Jane. 1991. "Grendel's Mother as Epic Anti-Type of the Virgin and Queen." In *Interpretations of Beowulf.* Ed. R. D. Fulk. Bloomington: Indiana University Press: 251-263.

Christian, Ed. 1978. "An Interview with John Gardner." In *Conversations with John Gardner*, edited Allan Chavkin. University of Mississippi Press, 1990), 183-203.

Cowart, David. 1983. *Arches & Light, The Fiction of John Gardner*. Carbondale: Southern Illinois University Press.

Diehl, Digby. 1971. "Medievalist in Illinois Ozarks." In *Conversations with John Gardner*, edited Allan Chavkin. University of Mississippi Press, 1990, 3-5.

Donaldson, E. Talbot *trans*. 1966. *Beowulf: a New Prose Translation*. New York: W.W. Norton.

Donelson, Ken. 1997. "'Filth' and 'Pure Filth' in Our Schools-Censorship of Classroom Books in the Last Ten Years." The English Journal 86.2 (Feb. 1997): 21-25. JSTOR. The Catholic University of America, Washington, D.C. 5 Jan. 2008.

Ellis, Helen B. and Warren U. Ober. 1982. "*Grendel* and Blake: The Contraries of Existence." *John Gardner, Critical Perspectives*. Eds.

Robert A. Morace and Kathryn VanSpanckeren. Carbondale: Southern Illinois University Press, 46-61.

Fawcett, Barry, and Elizabeth Jones. 1990. "The Twelve Traps in John Gardner's *Grendel.*" *American Literature* 62, no. 4: 634–47. https://doi.org/10.2307/2927072.

Ferguson, Paul F., John R. Maier, Frank McConnell, and Sara Matthiessen. 1977. "John Gardner: The Art of Fiction LXXIII." In *Conversations with John Gardner*, edited Allan Chavkin. University of Mississippi Press, 1990), 143-171.

Gardner, Joel. 2009. Interviewed by author. Susquehanna, PA: Annual John Gardner Conference.

Gardner, John. 1970. *The Complete Works of the Gawain Poet*. Carbondale: Southern Illinois University Press.

Gardner, John. 1975. *The Construction of Christian Poetry in Old English*. Carbondale: Southern Illinois University Press.

Gardner, John and Lewis Dunlap, eds. 1962. *The Forms of Fiction, an Anthology*. New York: Random House.

Gardner, John. 1970. "Fulgentius's Expositio Vergiliana Continentia and the Plan of *Beowulf*: Another Approach to the Poem's Style and Structure." *Papers on Language and Literature*, 6: 227-62.

Gardner, John and John Maier, *ed.* and *trans.* 1984. *Gilgamesh*. New York: Knopf.

Gardner, John. 1971. *Grendel*. New York: Vintage Press.

Gardner, John. 1983. *On Becoming a Novelist*. New York: Harper and Row.

Gardner, John. 1978. *On Moral Fiction.* New York: Basic Books.

Goldsmith, M.E. 1962. "Christian Perspective in *Beowulf*." Comparative Literature 14.1 (Winter 1962): 71-90.

Green, Martin. 1994. "Man, Time, and Apocalypse in *The Wanderer*, *The Seafarer*, and *Beowulf*." In *Old English Shorter Poems*, ed. Katherine O'Brien O'Keeffe. New York: Garland Publishing.

Harvey, Marshall L. 1977. "Where Philosophy and Fiction Meet, an Interview with John Gardner." In *Conversations with John Gardner*, edited Allan Chavkin. University of Mississippi Press, 86-98.

Henderson, Jeff. 1985. "John Gardner's Layered Fiction: The Supernatural and the Paranatural." In *Thor's Hammer: Essays on John Gardner*, eds. Jeff Henderson, Leonard C. Butts, Kathryn Van Spanckeren. Conway: University of Central Arkansas Press:167-180.

Howell, John M. 1980. *John Gardner: A Bibliographic Profile.* Carbondale: Southern Illinois University Press.

Howell, John M. 1993. *Understanding John Gardner*. Columbia: USC Press.

Kiessling, Nicolas K. 1968. "Grendel: A New Aspect." *Modern Philology* 65.3 (Feb. 1968): 191-201.

Klinkowitz, Jerome. 1981. "John Gardner's *Grendel*." *John Gardner, Critical Perspectives*. Morace and VanSpankeren 62-67.

Koberl, Johann. 2002. *The Indeterminacy of Beowulf*. Lanham: University Press of America.

Lawrence, William Witherle. 1967. *Beowulf and Epic Tradition*. New York: Hafner.

LeClair, Thomas. 1978. "William Gass and John Gardner: A Debate on Fiction." In *Conversations with John Gardner*, edited Allan Chavkin. University of Mississippi Press, 1990. 172-182.

Lewis, Theodore J. 1996. "CT 13.33-34 and Ezekiel 32: Lion-Dragon Myths." *Journal of the American Oriental Society* 116.1 (Jan. - Mar. 1996): 28-47.

McNamee, M.B. 1991. "*Beowulf*—An Allegory of Salvation?" In *Interpretations of Beowulf. ed.* R.D.Fulk. Indiana University Press, 1991.88-102.

Morace, Robert A. and Kathryn VanSpanckeren, *eds.* 1982. *John Gardner, Critical Perspectives*. Carbondale: Southern Illinois University Press.

Morris, Gregory. 1984. *A World of Order and Light: The Fiction of John Gardner*. Athens: University of Georgia Press.

Nutter, Ronald. 1997. *A Dream of Peace: Art and Death in the Fiction of John Gardner*. New York: Peter Lang.

Orchard, Andy. 2003. *A Critical Companion to Beowulf*. Cambridge: D.S. Brewer, 2003.

Orchard, Andy. 1995. *Pride and Prodigies: Studies in the Monsters of the Beowulf-Manuscript*. Cambridge: D.S. Brewer, 1995.

Phillpotts, Bertha S. 1928. "Wyrd and Providence in Anglo-Saxon Thought." Reprinted from *Essays and Studies* 13 (1928), 7-27, in *Interpretations of Beowulf*, ed. Fulk, R.D., Bloomington and Indianapolis: Indiana University Press.

Reilly, Charlie. 1977. "A Conversation with John Gardner," *Conversations with John Gardner*. Edited Allan Chavkin. University of Mississippi Press, 1990, 50-83.

Risden, Edward L. 1994. *Beasts of Time: Apocalyptic Beowulf*. New York: Peter Lang.

Savini, Rachel E. 2019. "The —ick of It: Phalluses, Swords, and Character Development in *Beowulf* and *Morte d'Arthur*," *International Journal of Undergraduate Research and Creative Activities*, Vol. 11, Article 7. (2019) DOI: 10.7710/2168-0620.1135

Stromme, Craig J. 1978. "The Twelve Chapters of *Grendel*." *Critique: Studies in Modern Fiction* 20.1: 83-92.

Tolkien, J.R.R. "*Beowulf*: The Monsters and the Critics." *Proceedings of the British Academy*, 22 (1936): 245–95. Reprinted in *An Anthology of Beowulf Criticism*, ed. Lewis E. Nicholson. 1963. Notre Dame, Ind.: University of Notre Dame Press.

Trilling, Renee R. 2007. "Beyond Abjection: The Problem with Grendel's Mother Again." *Parergon* 24.1: 1-20. Project Muse. The Catholic University of America, Washington, D.C. Feb. 2008 j

Waller, Shane. 1992. *Beowulf: Introduction*. London: Dover Publications.

Whallon, William. 1962. "The Christianity of *Beowulf*." *Modern Philology* Vol. 60, No. 2. (Nov. 1962): 81-94. JSTOR. The Catholic University of America, Washington, D.C. Jan. 2007.

Winther, Per. 1982. *The Art of John Gardner*. Albany: SUNY Press.

Zeeman, Kenneth L. 1997. "Grappling with Grendel or What We Did When the Censors Came." *The English Journal* 86.2 (Feb. 1997): 46-49. JSTOR. The Catholic University of Arnerica, Washington, D.C. 22 Jan. 2008

Ziegler, Heide. 1978. "John Gardner." In *Conversations with John Gardner*, edited Allan Chavkin. University of Mississippi Press, 1990, 117-142.

* note that for the interviews found in the book *Conversations with John Gardner*, I've put the date the interview is said to have taken place just after the name of the interviewer, though I've left 1990 after the name of the press.